A Practical Guide to
Prosperous Living

A Practical Guide to
Prosperous Living

J. Douglas Bottorff

Unity Village, Missouri

First Edition 1998

To receive a catalog of all our Unity publications (books, cassettes, compact discs, and magazines) or to place an order, call the Customer Service Department: (816) 969-2069 or 1-800-669-0282.

Unity Books acknowleges these contributors to this book: Michael Maday, Raymond Teague, Cathy McKittrick, editorial; Kay Thomure, copyediting; Shari Behr, Deborah Dribben, proofreading; Rozanne Devine, production; Roger Hunt, book design; Allen Liles, Sharon Sartin, Karen King, marketing.

Cover design and art by Gail Ishmael

The Revised Standard Version is used for
all Bible verses, unless otherwise stated.

Library of Congress Cataloging-in-Publication Data
Bottorff, J. Douglas.
   A practical guide to prosperous living / J. Douglas Bottorff. —
1st ed.
       p.   cm.
   Includes bibliographical references.
   ISBN 0-87159-220-7
   1. Success—Religious aspects—Christianity.   2. Wealth—Religious
aspects—Christianity.   3. Unity School of Christianity—Doctrines.
I. Title.
BV4598.3.B68   1998
248.4'8997—DC21   97-52696
                                                                        CIP

Unity Books feels a sacred trust to be a healing presence in the world. By printing with biodegradable soybean ink on recycled paper, we believe we are doing our part to be wise stewards of our Earth's resources.

Dedication

This book is dedicated to Pat and Carl Bottorff, two wonderful parents who always encouraged me to be true to myself and to follow my dreams.

Table of Contents

Introduction

When I think back to the time, less than two years ago, when I first began to gather ideas for writing this book, I am amazed, almost astounded, by the changes that have transpired in my life. I attribute these changes to my making the ideas that I share in this book the absolute basis of my life.

The changes I am talking about have been wonderful changes, the kinds of changes one would hope to experience through the study of prosperity principles. If someone were to ask me what I would do to make my life better than it is right now, I would have to say, probably for the first time in my life, that I don't know how I could make it any better. My work as a minister is more fulfilling than ever. I am living out a longtime dream of writing books, sharing the message that has transformed my life. I am fulfilling another dream of writing, recording, and performing music with the same kind of transformative message. I have a wonderful marriage of twenty years that gets better with each passing year. To top it all off, I now live in what I think of as one of the most beautiful places in the nation.

These, of course, are external things, things that have been important parts of my life now for many years. But all of them have taken on new life and new dimensions as the direct result of what is happening within me. And this is the most exciting change of all. Something within me has solidified. I have experienced a very simple but very profound realization that has now become the basis from which I consciously and intentionally live my life.

In my quest for an understanding of the essential ingredients of a successful and prosperous life, I have come to realize that there are two fundamental requirements: *You must be true to your Self,* and *you must pursue your dreams.* To be true to your Self is to be true to God. To pursue your dreams is to do God's will. Everything else follows these two things.

A Practical Guide to Prosperous Living is my attempt to explain what I mean when I say that you must be true to your Self and you must pursue your dreams. It is also my attempt to explain how to do it. My friend and colleague Dr. George Hilbert was always fond of saying, "People would rather *see* a sermon than hear one." In this book I am taking his advice by sharing with you many examples drawn from my own life to illustrate my points. It is important to me that you know I, too, have encountered all the same kinds of struggles and grappled with the same kinds of difficult questions which almost everyone who embarks upon the spiritual path of prosperity encounters. Besides, I feel a little like Thoreau

when he wrote, "I should not talk so much about myself if there were anybody else whom I knew as well."[1]

It is my hope that through this sharing I can in
some way help encourage you to be true to yourself
and pursue your dreams until you, too, find yourself
living in the midst of a life which is everything you
want it to be. The way is not always easy. Self-honesty
will often be your only guide. You will be required to
confront all your worst fears. There will be times
when you will feel alone, afraid, perhaps abandoned.
There are no shortcuts to learning to be true to your
Self and to following your dreams. But the rewards
of doing so are immense, and they are within your
reach. When you agree to be true to your Self and
follow your dreams, you are agreeing to experience
a life of prosperity that exceeds your greatest ex-
pectations.

Chapter 1

The Essence of Prosperity

How It All Began

I do not remember exactly when I began in earnest my personal quest for a better understanding of prosperity. For a long time, I suppose, I was, like many, satisfied to assume that prosperity was a possession-based affair, consisting primarily of acquiring money and other things I did not have. I was excited by books that taught me how to use my powers of visualization, willpower, faith, and any social skills I might have to get the things I wanted out of life.

Through the use of the techniques taught in these various books, I have indeed managed to acquire and accomplish many things. What's more, I have come to realize that, armed with such tools, I can have and do just about anything I set my mind to. I have either accomplished or am in the process of accomplishing every major, heartfelt goal that I have set for myself.

In the meantime, however, I have learned something important about the experience of accomplishment and acquiring things. I have learned that they do not possess the power to enhance the way I feel about myself, at least not for long. I enjoy getting new things, probably as much as anyone. It's fun to buy new cars, new clothing, new computers, and any other useful gadgets that help to make daily life easier or more productive. But I have noticed that, within a few days of every new acquisition, I feel just about the same as I did before I got it. Yes, the new item may be useful. It may be a pleasure to own. But it soon becomes routine, even mundane, and I find myself taking it for granted. When the excitement of the newness wears off, I'm pretty much the same person I was before this thing came into my life.

I also find this to be true with making money. Today I make twice the money I did at one time. I'm sure in the past I dreamed of how wonderful life would be when I made the kind of money I do now. It wouldn't surprise me to find my current level of income on an old, yellowed dream list or an aged treasure map packed away in a box somewhere in the basement. But now that I make this amount of money, I don't seem to be all that different from what I was back then, at least not because of the money. Of course, it allows me to have and do things I once couldn't afford to have and do. But I've grown to accept this new amount, and frankly, though I bless and appreciate it, I'll have to admit that I take it for granted as well. So, in my quest for understanding prosperity, I have had to take this interesting phenomenon into consideration.

A Blasé Attitude
Toward Things Is Common

Now, if this reaction to material things were unique to me, I might not think much about it. But through my close interactions with people over the years, particularly in my role as minister and spiritual counselor, it seems that these feelings I've experienced toward material things are quite common. I've known people who were almost swimming in a sea of possessions but treated them as casually and as indifferently as if they didn't even exist. Having such an abundance of possessions certainly did not produce the freedom, peace of mind, or satisfaction they obviously lacked. And the inevitable question that would always arise in one form or another from those who were supposed to have it all was always the same: Why? These encounters, as well as my own feelings, remind me of a saying found in The Gospel of Thomas.[1] Here Jesus is quoted as saying, *"Oh Lord, there are many around the drinking trough, but there is nothing in the cistern."*[2]

Where Things Fit In

Obviously, the acquisition of things *does* factor into the prosperity issue. They are important. But they're important in a way that is probably different from what we generally suspect. The problem is that we have tried to make money, accomplishments, positions, and relationships induce in us a deep sense of satisfaction they simply do not have the capacity to deliver, at least not for long. We have looked to these things as our basis for self-esteem, security, prestige, power, and identity, to the extent that we have come to believe we are, as individuals, incomplete without them.

What Do We Hope to Find in Our Acquisitions?

What is it that motivates us to continue to accumulate these things that promise to enrich the way we feel about ourselves but seldom do? What is it that keeps us "around the drinking trough" even though we suspect the cistern is empty? What exactly is it that we are hoping to find in this empty cistern? The answer is simple. We are hoping to find our Self, the real, spiritual essence of us. Behind every single desire that we have is the deeper desire for Self-expression. Every external thing we want to bring into our life represents but a small facet of this Self that we can only unleash from within our own depths.

There is nothing wrong with acquiring or accomplishing things. But if these acquisitional activities are to produce the satisfaction we expect from them, *they must somehow serve the deeper, more fundamental process of Self-expression.* We cannot achieve the sense of completeness that we crave by attempting to fill the cistern from the exterior. We must learn to first tap the inner spring from which our being originates and, from this one eternal Source, fill both the interior and exterior aspects of our lives.

A Simple Message

The message of this book is simple. If you want a prosperous, happy, fulfilling life, there are two things that are required of you. You must learn to be true to your Self, and you must be involved in an active pursuit of the dreams of your heart. To be true to your Self is to live from that eternal, cosmic fountain of life welling up from within you, to live, as Emerson put it, with the privilege of "the immeasurable mind."[3] It is to be guided by your own inner counsel—to draw, from your own inner strength and power, the genuine, absolute conviction in the purpose and the absolute goodness of life. To follow your dreams is to employ your natural talents to express yourself in a particular manner that is unique, comfortable, and naturally interesting to you. It is to engage in a work which you love, a work which does not have you counting the hours before you can leave it, but has you lamenting over the fact there do not seem to be enough hours in the day to do all you want to do.

To engage in these two activities is the key to understanding prosperity. Until you make the accomplishment of these two objectives your sole mission in life, you will never attain the quality of experience you deeply crave.

You, like many other people, may be living under the false assumption that something in your external life has to change before you can show the world who you really are and before you can begin pursuing the life of your dreams. Something *does* have to change, of course. But that something is not, as you might suspect, your level of income, it's not the job you're in, it's not your spouse, and it's not the place you live. It is *you.* If you are unhappy with your life, then it is because you are, in a hundred different ways throughout your day, making the decision *not* to be true to your Self and *not* to follow your dreams. This unconscious denial of Self-expression is the only reason that you are not happy with your life.

It does not matter how good a person you try to

be. It does not matter how hard you work. It does not matter how much you accumulate in terms of material wealth. *"What does it profit them if they gain the whole world, but lose or forfeit themselves?"*[4] Until you decide to be true to your Self and to pursue your dreams, you will never tap into the full essence of prosperity that is available to you.

The Wise and Foolish Builders

Jesus referred to the importance of being true to your Self in his parable of the wise and foolish builders.[5] The wise builder *"dug deep, and laid the foundation upon rock; and when a flood arose, the stream broke against that house and could not shake it, because it had been well built."* The foolish man *"built a house on the ground without a foundation; against which the stream broke, and immediately it fell."*

The *foundation,* a key image in this parable, represents your true Self. The house is your external life. A life built upon the foundation of your true Self, which, in turn, rests upon the *rock* of the Infinite Presence, is a life that is stable, successful, fulfilling, and fruitful. Your true Self is the channel through which the Infinite expresses Itself. Your heartfelt dreams are the intended means you are to use to externalize your true Self. Therefore, you can render no greater service to God, to yourself, or to your world than to be true to your Self and to follow your dreams. This is what you and I are here to do, and until we approach the prosperity issue with this understanding, the rich and fulfilling life we deeply crave will remain elusive.

Not Always Easy

Regardless of where you are or what you are doing in life, you can begin now to discover and be true to your Self, and you can begin now to identify and follow your dreams. It will not always be easy, because it will require a complete shift in many of your basic beliefs, as well as much of your behavior. But, as I tell people all the time, it is easier than *not* doing it. If you've ever lived a mediocre life that is going nowhere, you know there is nothing easy about *that*. Among other things, living such a life requires a great deal of hard labor, a constant honing of your manipulative skills, participation in what often amounts to fierce competition, a prostitution of your creativity, a giving up of your peace of mind, and a sacrifice of your self-esteem. And for what? A life whose outcome you can predict thirty years down the road? Is this what you are on this planet to do? Is this the intended use of your creative imagination, your natural interests, your natural love for life? If you agree that it is not, then when will it all change? When you finally make enough money? When you finally surround yourself with enough things? When you finally win this rat race? If this is what you are waiting for, let me assure you that you will have better luck making your way to first-in-line in rush-hour traffic than you will in attaining the life of your dreams.

When you do begin to make a conscious effort to listen to your Self and to pursue the life dictated by your heart, your cup will begin immediately to fill to overflowing. You will love who you are, you will love what you do, and you will, by virtue of your contentment and natural enthusiasm for life, become an inspiration to those around you. In addition, you will draw to you the material things and conditions that allow you to, paraphrasing Thoreau, advance confidently in the direction of your dreams.[6] In short, you will understand and experience the essence of prosperity.

Summary

1. If I feel that accomplishments and things do not give me the satisfaction I desire, it is only because they do not have the *capacity* to give satisfaction.

2. What I am really looking for in my acquisitional activities is a deeper experience of my true Self.

3. I am happy to the degree that I am being true to my Self and am actively involved in the pursuit of my dreams. These two activities are the essence of all material prosperity.

4. The pursuit of being true to my Self and following my dreams may not always be easy, but it is easier than *not* doing it.

Chapter 2

The Foundation for Lasting Prosperity

A Lesson From a Flower

A number of years ago a woman decided to plant a circle of tulip bulbs around a tree on the church lawn. According to the nursery where she bought the bulbs, the tulips would all be red. I watched from the window of my office as the plants began to grow. Day after day they grew taller, eventually sending out their crimson blossoms for all the world to see. They were red indeed, just as the nursery said they would be—with the exception of one. One out of those hundred or so red tulips was yellow.

At first, the yellow tulip looked out of place and we considered uprooting it to keep the color uniform. But upon further consideration, we decided to leave it. We decided that the symbolism embodied in the yellow tulip had much to teach us. It certainly had much to teach *me.* As I observed this yellow tulip, the thought came to me that the tulip was making no excuses or apologies for being what it was. It stood as high and as proud as any of the red tulips surrounding it. In spite of the fact that it grew right in the midst of a sea of red tulips, it had decided to be the best yellow tulip it knew how to be.

What a profound lesson in individualism! There was nothing in this yellow tulip's makeup that would allow it to try to be something it was not. It would never have to struggle, as so many of us do, with the pain of thinking it should be one thing when it was really something else.

The Enticement of Conformity

We have all experienced, at least in some degree, the pain and discomfort that come from trying to be someone or something we are not. As children, our natural inclination is to express our individualistic nature, a fact that often gives rise to embarrassing occasions for any parent. It is something we do well from the time we are born to that time when we begin to become socially conscious. Then we tend to become very guarded about how we express ourselves, careful to do it in a way that will be acceptable to our peers. This usually becomes very pronounced in the young-adult years. The worst thing that can happen here is that you find you are a yellow tulip among a sea of red ones. Perhaps you still carry painful memories of those years when the need to fit in was particularly prevalent.

Through this period we are vulnerable to the enticements of conformity. It is a time when we begin to *wear* our identity, to don red garments to hide the yellow, to show the world where we stand by how we look and how well we can fit in. Some never grow out of this phase. They engage in an adult life of staged appearances of wealth, success, and happiness, while jockeying for positions of power and recognition at the office or the PTA, always putting public opinion of who they are ahead of how they actually feel about themselves. It is little wonder that Henry David Thoreau concluded that *"the mass of men lead lives of quiet desperation."*[1]

My Own Need to Fit In

These early years were certainly painful years for me. The small-town high school I attended was strongly centered around sports, football in particular. I tried to fit into my high school society by becoming a football player. It seemed that all the popular people were related to sports in one way or another. I was a gangly 120 pounds of complete physical uncoordination that could not even run and dribble a basketball at the same time, let alone remember how to run football plays. I dreaded the pain of football practice. I didn't even like the smell of the locker room.

My need to fit in kept me trying to be a football player from the seventh through the tenth grades. One day, after being knocked senseless while ramming another boy head on, I retired from my football career. It was an easy decision. When I recovered consciousness, I looked around and for a while, everything had a green cast to it. I decided it wasn't worth it, so I hung up my shoulder pads once and for all.

The Unnatural Mask of Personality

Our need to conform, to fit in, is a strong one indeed. No one wants to be left on the sidelines while the game is going on, whatever the game may be. And so we go to great lengths to make ourselves fit into social circles that are neither naturally interesting to us nor fitting to who we are. And because we fear that who we are will not fit in, we begin early to put aside our genuine thoughts and feelings, returning to them only in times when we are alone, free to relax our cumbersome facade. But because we believe it is this facade that makes us socially acceptable, we do not wish to relax it too much, lest we lose the social advantages we think it engenders. If

Thoreau's observation was correct, we could easily trace this desperation back to the struggle of maintaining an unnatural mask of personality. Certainly, each time I suited up in a football uniform, I began leading a life of quiet desperation. I may have looked like everyone else, but I felt like an alien.

That society, like most, did not encourage individualism. And, since football set the social standard, quitting the team essentially meant you were a social dropout. But drop out I did, and the experience helped me to begin to wake up to the need to listen to my own heart over the opinions of any given social circle.

Of Head-On Collisions and Value Systems

Have you ever noticed that it sometimes takes a few head-on collisions in life before you begin seriously to assess your shallow pride and ego-based system of values and to start making decisions from the heart, even if they are socially unpopular? It is amazing how one good bump on the head helped me sort out, in an instant, a struggle that had been going on for many of those early years. What a freeing realization it was to know that I did not have to be a football player anymore!

I am not making a case against high school football. I am talking about our tendency to create a self-image based more on popular social opinion than on the dictates of our own heart. I am talking about our tendency to override our real feelings for the sake of fitting in. This tendency, I believe, lies at the root of the majority of our problems when it comes to attaining a truly prosperous life. We try to operate successfully within a framework of success standards that have little to do with who and what we are at the deepest levels of our being. "We sell the thrones of angels," as Emerson wrote, "for a short and turbulent pleasure."[2]

Beyond the Dark Night

The truly prosperous life is not something we can acquire from the external world. It is something we must evolve from within ourselves. Each one of us is endowed with a high calling, a calling that may not be presently apparent to us in any form other than a sense of dissatisfaction with our life as it is. Dissatisfaction is always a signal that we are not living life to its fullest available potential, that we are somehow thwarting the expression of a quality of experience we know instinctively we can and should have. Dissatisfaction is, in fact, a path that, when traced back to its origins, will lead us both to our true Self and to an eternal set of values which eventually become a new basis for the life we know is possible.

The distance you must travel between the "place" you are now and the place you want to be may seem long and formidable and, at times, impossible to traverse. This idea is reflected in the lyrics of a song I wrote, *"Beyond the Dark Night of the Soul."*

There'll be times, on your journey
When you'll lose everything you've gained.
And your faith will start to waver
When it takes you just as far as it can go.
Then you let go—
    that you may live—
Till you see something of a beacon through
    the haze, through the haze.[3]

The "faith" which wavers is the faith which is based on appearances, personal power, and a false self-image. This faith *must* be forced beyond its limits and on into oblivion if we are to rest our convictions on that which is real and changeless. This is often a frightening and painful process, because, as we will see in a later chapter, it involves the death of an identity we have grown accustomed to. We will be tempted to turn away from this process many times.

From the night, the world calls your name,
And you turn to see if something's left behind.[4]

But this internal sorting-out process is the path to permanent prosperity, and we will return to it when we have, to our satisfaction, exhausted everything of lesser value.

> Then you know, there's nothing there for you,
> And you free another portion of your mind—
>   of your mind.[5]

From the Inside Out

What we are all looking for is the correct way that we, as human beings, can flourish on this planet. As presumptuous as this may sound, there is, by natural design, only one way that this can happen with any sense of permanency: this way is *from the inside out.* Each one of us is the product of a Cosmic activity that is creating individualized expressions of Itself from an invisible blueprint. This blueprint is implanted at the core of the individual and is that individual's essential nature. It is our true Self, our spiritual essence, and it must be factored into everything we do if we are to be successful. If this Self goes unacknowledged, either through ignorance or through fear, then discomfort and dissatisfaction set in. We feel inadequate and we come to know lack.

As a football player I experienced deep feelings of lack and inadequacy, feelings I may never have come to know so intimately had I never suited up for that particular sport. And what did I try to do to compensate for these negative feelings? Instead of listening to my heart, I tried to become a better football player. This was exactly the *wrong* thing to do. But I have discovered that we do not usually question and change our dysfunctional goals and behaviors until we are completely satisfied they hold nothing of value for the advancement of our soul. We may, in fact, return to them many times before we finally abandon them. Then when we do abandon them, we do so from a true knowledge base, rather than because we read we were supposed to.

Trying to Fit In

One important observation I have gleaned from my football endeavors and other, similar experiences is that my feelings of lack and inadequacy were there, not because I was lacking and inadequate as a person, but because I was lacking and inadequate as a football player. There is a tremendous difference. I was trying to fit into the world as one thing when I was, in fact, something entirely different.

Based on my years spent as the minister and proponent of a spiritual philosophy in which the concept of prosperity plays such an important role, I have concluded: *What many people are actually trying to accomplish in their quest for a more prosperous life is to eradicate feelings of lack and inadequacy that have arisen because they are trying to relate to the world as one thing when they are, in fact, something quite different.* From this point of view, prosperity is something that is defined more out of a reactive sense of inadequacy than out of a creative means of actually advancing the natural, expansive impulse of the soul. The result of pursuing a prosperous life based on such an erroneous premise is that in so doing we actually strengthen our sense of inadequacy, rather than eliminate it.

When I was trying to fit into my high school society, for example, I would have defined prosperity as anything that would help make me a better football player. My motivation to prosper was a negative one, based on the attempt to compensate for my feelings of inadequacy. When my oldest brother ordered a Charles Atlas muscle-building course, I knew my prosperity was finally on its way. In just a few short weeks, I would have the physique that would not only make a football star out of me, but also make me one of the most sought-after members of my high school society! Well, the course did come, and it didn't take long to realize that if I was going to look like Charles Atlas, I would have to make that the entire object of my existence—forever! The short time I did devote myself to the course showed no visible signs of progress, so I quit. So much for mail-order muscles! Had I chosen to proceed, I actually would have prospered myself further and further away from my more natural, yet still unrecognized talents.

Be True to Your Self

I can say, without hesitation, that the one most important guiding principle to successful living I have tried to instill in my two children is to *be true to your Self*. Through their high school years, I have watched them go through their own struggles with the pressure to conform. Like any caring parent, I have offered what I have gleaned from my own awkward and insecure years, only to be rebuffed with this: "Things are different now, Dad. It's a lot more complicated now than when you were a kid." In some ways this is true. But the essential Truth will always remain the same. If you want to be successful and prosper through life, regardless of the type of social milieu you are in, you must listen to and be true to your Self. What you are at the deepest level of your being is designed for success. You are a cosmic being that transcends all the petty fears and insecurities inherent in those who build their identities upon the shifting sands of fad, fashion, and social popularity. You are not here to conform, but to awaken to your inner flame of individuality, to let this flame rise and shine through you in a way that only you can.

A Lesson From *The Ugly Duckling*

Let's go a step further. The good news is that on a cosmic scale, you cannot *not* be true to yourself! That inner flame of individuality must awaken, as we see so clearly in Hans Christian Andersen's famous tale, *The Ugly Duckling*. This simple story has profound implications for living our lives.

You recall the tale about a young swan that is born and raised with ducks. Other animals make fun of him and say he is ugly, because he does not look like them. The little swan is hurt, confused, and dejected. One day he sees a group of marvelous swans and instinctively feels close to them. With a change of seasons, the ugly duckling, of course, turns into a beautiful swan.

The moral of Andersen's poignant tale is that ultimately you must be true to your Self. You can take detours against your nature, either through choices (becoming a football player) or circumstances (being raised in a family of ducks), and travel some rather rocky and unsatisfying roads, but you *will* come back to a remembrance of your true, essential nature. The ugly duckling experiences an innate longing for the Self and finds happiness only when he lives from his true nature. An important point for us to keep in mind is that the swan's transformation—his inner awakening—comes naturally, in due course. Because God has designed you for success, the Self—in divine order—will shine forth.

Summary

1. The reason I experience dissatisfaction in my life is that I am not being true to my Self.

2. The "head-on collisions" I experience can help me wake up to the importance of being true to my Self.

3. I cannot acquire a prosperous life from the external world. I must evolve it from within myself. I am designed to prosper *from the inside out.*

4. My feelings of lack and inadequacy come from trying to be something that I am not.

5. The most important thing I can do in life is to be true to my Self.

Chapter 3

The Law of Infinite Expansion

Grasping the Idea

I discovered long ago that there is a vast difference between being exposed to an idea and having
that idea become an integral aspect of my consciousness. This was especially true when it came to
thinking of myself as a spiritual being. I found that
trying to balance my personal, worldly affairs with
the idea I was an unlimited expression of the Infinite
often created perceptual conflicts in my daily life
which were difficult to explain, let alone resolve.

I didn't have any difficulty thinking of myself as a
spiritual being. I had, in fact, begun to experience this
aspect of myself in my more productive periods of
meditation. It was not even very difficult to grasp the
idea that prosperity begins on the spiritual level. But
still it was difficult to understand how I could trans-
late this wonderful information into applicable forms
that could be used in the pursuit of my dreams. There
seemed to always exist a frustratingly wide chasm be-

tween my newly emerging idealism and the mundane
challenges I faced in everyday living.

Reading and Doing

Having had the opportunity over the years to work
with countless people on their own quest for spiritual understanding, I have found such a chasm to be
a challenge that is common to many. When we get
fired up by a new idea we read or hear about, most
of us want to see immediate benefits of that idea in
our experience—especially when it concerns the
subject of prosperity. And yet, because of the seemingly slow nature of our evolutionary process, it may
be some time, perhaps years, before our lives begin
to reflect, to any great degree, the possibilities we
are able to grasp in an instant. At one time in my
spiritual journey, this bit of information would have
been discouraging to me. But the more I have
learned to accept it as a fact, the more relaxed I am
with my own evolutionary process.

I bring up this idea because of our tendency to
think it is the next book or the next seminar that is
going to change our lives. I once did a seminar on
my book *A Practical Guide to Meditation and Prayer.*
At the break a woman came up to me and expressed
disappointment that she felt no closer to a deep
meditative experience than she had before she at-

tended the class. I told her she would not get this type of experience either in a seminar or in a book on meditation. The only way she would get it, I said, was to meditate.

Everything we read and hear that is of a Truth-based nature is good and will, in some degree, influence our lives for the better. Like most people, I have always loved the experience of acquiring a new inspirational book, one that is difficult to put down at night and so easy to pick up the first thing in the morning. Such books become gentle and encouraging companions throughout our day. When things look bleak, we think about some meaningful idea we read, and that thought sparks a soothing glow of hope in us. We find ourselves looking forward to those next free moments when we can again crawl back into our book, which has become like a warm, comforting blanket to us.

The ability of certain authors to lift our hopes to the possibility of an immediately better life can actually produce in us a type of addiction that is difficult to break. I have noticed there are people who apparently consume such books for the "high" they induce, and yet acquire, in their quest for a better life, little more than a huge library. In spite of exposure to the potentially transforming knowledge contained in their books, these people continue their struggle through life.

New Thought pioneer H. Emilie Cady obviously observed this same phenomenon, for it prompted her to advise her readers to "stop reading many books."[1] She was not opposed to people furthering their education. She was simply advocating that people move past the opinions and experiences of others and dare to move into their own. She recognized that the inspiration we get from others, as alluring and as helpful as it may be, is short-lived. We must find our own light.

There is a time to read, of course. When I first discovered the Unity way of life, I could not read enough. I literally consumed every metaphysical book I could get my hands on. Looking back, I can see that it was a time of intellectual preparation, an important time of planting new seed ideas. But the time came when books no longer satisfied my hunger for a better life. They no longer sparked in me that "high" I so enjoyed. It was time to realize that if I wanted my life to change, I would have to face the stark realities I found there and apply what I knew to transform them into what I wanted.

The Living Force

At one particularly frustrating point in my life, a point when I was coming to the end of my book-consuming period, I experienced a very valuable revelation. I began to ask myself what it was in me that kept me pressing forward. What was it that caused me to do things like read these books, begin attending Unity churches, and go so far as question the authority of the conventional thinking of my upbringing and even my religious training? I started to realize that there was something, a *living force,* behind my desire to live a freer, more expanded, and more prosperous life. Whatever this *something* was, it was a living, ever-present, and very persistent aspect of my being that had been with me for as long as I could remember. It was a constant, though sometimes annoying, companion that would not leave me alone.

Gradually I began to follow Cady's advice, turning my attention from continual reading to acknowledging and observing this persistent inner activity. In periods of meditation I would practice feeling this inner *impulse* and try to understand what it was and where it was coming from. In time I realized that this impulse was definitely not of my own making. Its presence did not depend on my studying and understanding metaphysical principles. It was there, like some form of self-sustaining conscience that would not go away.

This impulse, I observed, was expansive in nature, in that it always projected in me a message of abundance, prompting me to desire a freer, less encumbered, and more prosperous life. My personal desire for a more prosperous life, I discovered, was actually my *response* to this unsolicited, expansive impulse. I have since labeled this natural phenomenon as the *impulse to prosper* and have come to realize it is universal, something that is shared by all people and all living things.

From Abstract to Familiar

As simple as it sounds, acknowledging the presence of this natural impulse to prosper proved to be a major spiritual breakthrough for me. This acknowledgment has helped me bring my spirituality down from an abstract concept into a very real and familiar influence in my daily life. Too often, I think, our spirituality remains an abstraction, a vague image we carry in our heads, something we contemplate when we're not busy dealing with the distractions of daily living. Our spirituality may, in fact, be such an abstraction to us that we believe we will have to study for years before we can understand it. This is simply not so.

Actually it is the fact that this impulse is so near and so familiar to us that we have overlooked it as the "still small voice" we read about in the Bible and in much of our metaphysical literature. This is precisely the problem with intellectualizing spiritual matters. The things that are this accessible and familiar to us, we reason, must not be the same things our favorite authors are writing about. The "voice" they speak of has to be something different than this expansive impulse we have felt all our life. Otherwise, our life would already be more like the ones these authors tend to describe in their books.

The Voice of God

This type of reasoning causes us to look for things foreign to the natural guidance system we have already come to know. Every time you do anything with the intention of establishing greater freedom in your life, you are responding—unconsciously perhaps—to the very voice of God speaking through you. Have you ever wondered why you desire such a life? Your impulse to prosper is nothing less than the voice of God urging you on to a freer, more expanded level of expression. The key is to *become conscious* of this impulse, recognize it for what it is, and learn to act on the guidance it is providing.

The Law of Infinite Expansion

Our desire to live a full, limitation-free, meaningful, creatively productive, and prosperous life is not something that originates at the personal level of our being. This desire is the effect of what Charles Fillmore described as the "law of infinite expansion." He defined this law as "the principle of never-ceasing growth and development toward the fulfillment of God's perfect idea that is firmly fixed in all creation."[2]

There is, within each of us, a "perfect idea" that is asserting itself as our impulse to prosper. The word *desire* comes from the Latin prefix *de-*, meaning "from," and *sidus,* meaning "star." *Desire* literally means "from the stars." The implication here is that desire is a *cosmic* impulse. Behind every specific desire we have, as elevated or as crude as it may be, lies the cosmic impulse to expand, to develop, as Fillmore stated, "toward the fulfillment of God's perfect idea that is firmly fixed in all creation."

Of course, this does not mean that every specific desire you have is itself cosmically sanctioned. If you do not understand your relation to the Whole and Its intention to expand through you, you will entertain many desires that represent little more than a blind groping after something you do not comprehend. This, in fact, is what I have come to see as the primary source of frustration that we often experience in our attempts to live a prosperous life. We have so misunderstood and personalized this law of infinite expansion, this impulse to prosper, that we have needlessly forced ourselves into an unnaturally laborious manifestation process which never was intended to be a part of the human experience.

Prosperity: An Inevitable Consequence of Your Spiritual Evolution

Because so many people have unknowingly relegated themselves to prospering by the sweat of their brow, they have developed an attitude that questions whether or not it is right for them to prosper. If you are one such person, your confusion will clear when you understand that your impulse to prosper does not originate with you. It is, rather, a natural, cosmic impulse that you are responding to. You *aspire* to better, freer conditions in life because you are *inspired* by the expansive intention of the Cosmos.

When Jesus said, "Seek first his kingdom and his righteousness, and all these things shall be yours as well,"[3] he was pointing out that the condition we describe as material prosperity is *the natural result of spiritual understanding.* If we do not understand ourselves and our desires in relation to the creative intention of God, we blindly flail about, laboring to establish conditions that would otherwise naturally occur with little or no effort on our part. In short, *a materially prosperous life is the natural and inevitable consequence of your spiritual evolution.*

If we are to truly understand the essence of prosperity, we have to free ourselves from the thought that our desire to prosper is merely a personal and selfish one. We must begin to see it as divine in nature, a universal rising of the creative life force attempting to do its expansive work through us. Making this shift from a personal to a more impersonal view of our impulse to prosper helps us to align ourselves with the universal creative flow that eventually unfolds as the life we know intuitively we can have.

Something to Do

In your quiet time, become aware of your own impulse to prosper, that compelling force in you which urges you forward, even in this moment as you read these words. As you observe it, free yourself of all responsibility for this impulse, this desire to expand into a freer, more prosperous life. Recognize that it is there as a self-sustaining, loving force, the "still small voice" of God speaking to you, a gentle presence urging you on. Allow yourself to stop trying so desperately to make things happen. Know that your desire for greater good is God's desire for you, that a "perfect idea" of greater good is now unfolding through you. Agree to let it happen. Agree to let God show you the way.

Affirmations

You can reinforce this realization through the use of the following affirmations:

- *My desire to grow, my impulse to prosper, is God desiring to expand through me.*

- *My desire and God's desire are one and the same.*

- *I am already familiar with God's voice speaking through me.*

- *I am already responding to God's voice speaking through me.*

- *I am now ready to release all my limited attempts to prosper and let God reveal to me what I should be doing.*

Summary

1. There is a "living force" within me that is prompting me to expand into a higher quality of life. This force is the voice of God.

2. The source of all my desires to live a freer life can be traced to the "law of infinite expansion: the principle of never-ceasing growth and

development toward the fulfillment of God's perfect idea that is firmly fixed in all creation." There is, within me, a "perfect idea" that is asserting itself as my impulse to prosper. My desire to prosper is the result of this "idea" asserting itself through me.

3. At the heart of all my desires is the cosmic desire to expand. Material prosperity is the natural result of my understanding of and cooperation with this cosmic desire.

Chapter 4

Pursuing Your Passion

A Right Vocation

In a televised interview with Bill Moyers, the late mythologist Joseph Campbell shared a phrase that struck a nerve in me and apparently in thousands of other people across our nation. If you want to be happy, he said, you have to "follow your bliss." Two implications that had special meaning for me are embodied in this statement. First, Campbell was saying that there is a right vocation for each person, a "bliss," something each of us loves to do and is able to do well. Second, if we are to live a happy, well-balanced, prosperous life, we have a spiritual obligation to pursue that vocation.

In reflecting on my personal reaction to Campbell's simple admonition to "follow your bliss," I realize it was so meaningful to me because it is the same message that has always been embodied in my own natural impulse to prosper. *Follow your bliss* is, I believe, a message from the heart of us all, a message we heard in some form long before it bubbled forth from the lips of Joseph Campbell.

I have come to believe that people inspire us because they articulate what we already know at the deepest levels of our being, all the more reason for learning to listen to our own prospering impulse. I have also discovered that any true success we experience in life does not come by merely nodding in agreement with what these inspiring people say. Our success comes as we express the courage to embody, in our own voice and in our own actions, that which we deeply know to be true.

Vocational Guidance

As discussed in the previous chapter, our impulse to prosper is the source of our desire to live a freer, more expansive life. But it is more. Within this natural impulse, there also exists the guidance toward a *particular vocational environment,* a type of work that will best serve the expressive needs of our emerging Self.

I discovered this vocational guidance in my own meditative process. I say, without any hesitation whatsoever, that my choice to enter a ministerial career unfolded from within me. It was not a choice I made based on family prompting or even on a particular interest I had in the profession. In fact, the ministry would have been one of the last choices I would have made, from an intellectual standpoint. The stereotypical image I carried of the people who chose the ministry as a profession was not an elevated one, to say the least. And yet the emerging new dimensions of my higher Self dictated clearly that the ministry was indeed the most suitable vocational environment for me.

I remember, while attending classes at Unity Village, Missouri, sitting on the patio drinking a cup of coffee and contemplating my future. I was frustrated with what I was doing and the direction my life was going. In this soul-searching moment, I asked myself what I would really like to do, what interested me the most. The answer came quickly. The thing I loved the most, the thing that was always on my mind, the thing I was devoting all my spare time to exploring, was my own developing spirituality. I was completely captivated by this new dimension that was unfolding from within. I wanted to do something that allowed me to devote all my time and energy to furthering this inner process and to sharing it with others. The ministry became the logical answer. Time has proven that it was the *right* answer.

The Lesson From the Sunflower

The invisible blueprint of our being, our true, spiritual Self, is communicating to our conscious mind, through our natural interests, desires, and talents, the way we can best express this higher Self in our daily life. Our vocation is to our spiritual identity what a proper growing environment is to a seed. If the seed is not dropped into the correct growing environment, its potential will remain untapped. It will either die or produce only a hint of its capacity. This fact was graphically illustrated the year my wife decided to plant sunflowers.

Using seeds from the same package, she planted them on both the north and south sides of our home. The ones on the south side, the side that received the most sunlight, grew to over 7 feet in height, producing heads that were so heavy with new seed that they literally bowed under their own weight. The plants that grew on the north side, however, grew to heights of only 2 to 3 feet, miniature daisy-like replicas of their southern counterparts.

There are many who are in "north-side" type jobs and careers, doing work that allows them to express only a fraction of who they are. It is said that we are to bloom where we are planted, that we are to learn to live as fully as possible right where we are in life. This is excellent advice that is, unfortunately, frequently misinterpreted. It means that we are to *begin* where we are, but not necessarily *stay* where we are. If what you are doing vocationally is not an extension of who you are at the deepest level, if you do not love and have total interest in what you do, you will never fully invest yourself in your work. You may, like the north-side sunflowers, bloom into something that resembles who you are. You may become monetarily successful, gleaning all kinds of prestige and benefits along the way. But you will never completely arouse your creative and expressive potential until you do the kind of work that reflects your deepest interests. Bloom where you are planted, yes. But the real key to successful living is to work toward planting yourself where you will bloom biggest and best.

Three Categories of Workers

It seems that there are three general categories of people found in the workplace. There are people who tolerate their work. There are people who like their work. And there are people who have a passion for their work.

The people who tolerate their work do so basically because it puts a roof over their head and food on their table. They usually maintain a very impersonal, often resentful attitude toward what they do, investing little more than their time in the job. I remember meeting a man at a wedding reception who had recently retired after working for a company for forty-two years. In the course of our conversation, he informed me that he absolutely hated every day he spent on that job. When I asked him why he kept at it for so long, his curt response was, "A man's gotta eat!" It is indeed a proven fact that we have to eat if we want to remain in our physical bodies. Knowing there is so much more to our presence here on this planet than to simply sustain a body, I could not help feeling saddened that this man had just spent forty-two years of his life merely addressing his needs.

A Revealing Poll

I recently read of a poll whose results revealed that the majority of the fifteen hundred people polled actually liked their jobs. This, to me, was a refreshing bit of information. The study showed that the primary reason they liked them, however, was because of the comfortable, more expanded lifestyle their jobs afforded them. In other words, this group of people liked what their jobs gave them more than they liked the jobs themselves. They were happy with the money and benefits the jobs provided, but the jobs did not represent a field of interest they would pursue if these benefits were removed. They were not unhappy with what they were doing for a living, but they were not passionate about it either. This category of people, the largest in the workplace, according to the poll, reminds me of the hamster running on the exercise wheel. If the hamster weren't in the cage, it probably wouldn't run on the wheel. There are many other things it would rather be doing.

Vocational Passion

The third category of people, those who are following their bliss, those who are passionate about their vocational choices, represents the happiest, most well-balanced, creatively exciting people you can meet. Having been through all three categories, I can tell you from experience that this third category is worth every ounce of energy you put into attaining it.

I have had jobs that I literally could not stand. I have taken other jobs with pleasant working conditions and salaries that provided me enough money to do some of the things I wanted, but I had no interest in the job itself. Now I am absolutely passionate about my work. Actually, I have three passions, all of which I am actively pursuing within the context of my ministry. I love to write, record, and perform music. I love to write books. And I love to teach people, through public speaking, how to get in touch with their spiritual nature and allow themselves to be transformed from the inside out.

When I get up in the morning, I do not go to an office and punch a time clock and then watch that clock for eight hours waiting until it is time to go home. In fact, I forget there *is* a clock. I may start working on a book or an album or a talk at six in the morning and then realize by two that afternoon I have not eaten anything yet! I become so engrossed in what I am doing that I don't think about anything else. A twelve- to fourteen-hour workday is not at all unusual for me. If this sounds like a symptom of a workaholic, it could be. But when your work is the thing you love doing most, then all the so-called normal standards we apply to our work habits fly right out the window. There is no difference between what I do for a living and who I am as a person.

What's more, at the risk of sounding like I'm bragging, people constantly thank me for doing what I love to do. I have a box filled with hundreds of letters from people all over the world thanking me for doing what I do. They also call me from all over the country with the same message. The satisfaction I get from this response is immeasurable, because it says to me that, aside from the personal gratification

I get from pursuing and expressing the things I am passionate about, I am also providing the greatest service I can possibly render to the rest of the world as well. It's a win/win situation.

Where Is Your Heart?

The ministry and all that implies is fitting for me, but it may not be fitting for you. You may have a passion for sales, architecture, art, travel, or one of any number of things. I recently met a man who fishes for trout for a living. Outdoor magazines hire him to travel to the most beautiful spots in the American West, fish for a few days, take pictures of the area, and write about the experience. This is his passion, because he told me he would be doing it whether or not he got paid. "I found myself sneaking off and fishing these mountains in all my spare moments," he said. "It hit me one day that this is where my heart is and this is what I should be doing all the time. I made the decision to figure out how to do it for a living."

The key to his statement was, "This is where my heart is." Your heart already knows what you should be doing. It is only a matter of your agreeing to do it and then taking the necessary steps that will open before you.

Commitment to Work

Let me warn you now, however, that things are not going to just fall into your lap. I believe that all people who are engaged in doing, as a vocation, what they love and do best have made a conscious decision to do so. I also believe that this decision involves a total commitment to working hard, to making various forms of sacrifice, and to forcing themselves to push past all their deepest fears. These are people who pressed on in spite of the fact they had moments when they began to believe that accomplishing their dream was something too good to be true. They are people who know what it is to awaken in a cold sweat at three o'clock in the morning, terrified by their own audacity to have struck out in this direction. They are people who have waited patiently in jobs and situations they did not like while some new phase of their dream unfolded, probably in a way they could not have foreseen. They are people who know what it feels like to wander aimlessly through long stretches of barren desert, not knowing when and where the next oasis may be. In other words, people who are now doing what they love to do in life have made the decision to meet and surmount every obstacle that stood between where they were and where they wanted to be. The same will be true with *anyone* who makes such a decision.

The pursuit of your passion will, as we will talk about in a later chapter, stir in you every fear, every self-imposed limitation, every self-doubt, every feeling of inadequacy that you harbor. You will not cease one day doing what you don't like and begin the next doing what you love. You will slowly evolve toward this new direction.

Some would look at my life and say that the Universe has blessed me with special treatment. I would be quick to disagree. In the first place, about seventeen years have passed since I decided what I would do with my life, and I feel as if I am only just now hitting my stride. The Universe has only responded to the decisions I have made to find and devote myself to doing, for a living, what I love and do best. I have experienced all the failure, disappointment, frustration, and fear that everyone who goes this way will encounter.

Much to Learn

There is a great deal to learn, or unlearn, about living the life of your dreams. The moment you agree that you are ready to learn, life begins presenting you with a series of tailor-made lessons designed to help you evolve from where you are to where you want to be. Some of these lessons will frighten you, some will anger you, some will disappoint you, some will elate you. All will advance you, though you may not see how at the time. It is a process similar to the one described by the sculptor who was asked how he carved an angel out of stone. "It's simple," he said. "You just chip away everything that doesn't look like an angel." There may be a lot in your life that doesn't look like the things you are passionate about. But there is a reason they are there, a sustaining factor that no doubt can be traced back to some aspect of your self-image. You will be given as many opportunities as you need to confront and eliminate this sustaining factor, and in so doing you will move that much closer to the life of your dreams.

Three Musts

Legend has it that when Socrates was asked for directions on how to get to Mount Olympus, his response was, "Just make sure that every step you take is in the direction of Mount Olympus." In giving concrete directions on how to begin doing what you love to do with your life, I feel I can only respond with the same kind of general advice. It involves changing the entire way you think about yourself and about your life. I will say there are three guiding principles, or "musts," that are followed by all who live the kind of life they love:

- There are no quick fixes to getting there, so you must commit yourself to the long haul.

- You must begin now making decisions and taking actions that support your dreams. You will never simply dream your dreams into reality.

- You must be willing to confront and eliminate the fears that would keep you from moving forward.

I will discuss in detail each of these ideas throughout the rest of this book, so please bear with the present generality. Following your bliss, pursuing your passion, heading for your particular Mount Olympus has to become a way of life. If you are not doing it now, that means your current way of life has to be abandoned and your desired way of life developed. The implications here run very, very deep. There will be days when you will take baby steps, days when you will take great strides, and days when you will think you are walking backwards. But when you agree to follow your dreams, you are agreeing to let the Universe begin Its wonderful work of pouring through you such a bounty of good that there will not be room enough in your life to receive it. It will spill out into the world as rich blessings for all who come into contact with it.

One Final Word

Before closing this chapter, I want to address one final, but very important, question raised by a woman in a class I was teaching one evening. Her question was this: "What do you do if you don't have a passion? What if you don't know what it is you want to do with your life?" I offered her this suggestion: Turn your focus away from finding something you can get passionate about, and focus more on Self-discovery through meditation. The reason you do not know what you want to do with your life is that it is not yet clear to you who you are at the deepest levels of your being. You must learn to go within yourself and discover your own essence before you can take the next step of expressing that essence in a given vocational direction. My choice to enter the ministry was not, as I said, one that was based on intellectual reasoning. It was the direct result of Self-discovery through meditation. Your spiritual essence will dictate to you the way it can and should best be expressed.

Summary

1. There is a right vocation for me. If I am to be happy and express all that is in me, I have a spiritual obligation to pursue it.

2. There is vocational guidance in the meditative process. As I go within, I am guided into the best vocation.

3. My current work may put a roof over my head, but if I am not passionate about it, it is not the best thing I could be doing.

4. Doing what I love to do will require a great deal from me. But the rewards of doing it will far outweigh any struggle I encounter.

5. I realize there are no quick fixes to getting where I want to be in life. I realize I must begin now to make decisions that support my dreams. I realize I must confront and release all fears that arise as I move closer to the life of my dreams.

6. If I do not have a particular passion I wish to pursue, I will focus my attention on Self-discovery through meditation, knowing that my natural desires and talents will arise through knowing my true Self.

Chapter 5

Understanding Your Motivation to Prosper

Who Is This *You*?

The obvious question most of us would like an answer to when we pick up a prosperity-based book such as this one, is: *How do I become prosperous?* A significantly more important question, however, is this: *Who is this I whom I am trying to prosper?* Are you trying to prosper the true, spiritual being which you are, or are you trying to prosper the limited self-image which you *think* you need to be? Is it your objective to express all the innate splendor of the *swan* that you are? Reaching a clear understanding of your motivation to prosper may be one of the most significant breakthroughs you make when it comes to living a truly prosperous life. Why? Because when you know what it is you are actually trying to achieve, your efforts will be focused and you will achieve it.

It has been my observation that, in our quest for a more prosperous life, many of us are motivated by the need to compensate for feelings of personal lack and inadequacy, feelings which, as I discovered in my short-lived high school football career, can only be eradicated by drawing from the well of our own spiritual resources. I know that in those early high school years I felt incomplete as a person. In my quest for prosperity, I was really looking for things that would make me feel better about myself and allow me to fit in. My motive to prosper was negative, compensatory in nature. When this is the case, no external acquisition is satisfying, because nothing external has the ability to compensate for that which we feel we lack as a person.

Conclusionistic Thinking

The thinking that stems from this belief that external things and accomplishments can compensate for feelings of personal inadequacy is what I have come to call *conclusionistic thinking*. The logic of the conclusionistic thinker would go like this: My quest for happiness, peace of mind, freedom, satisfaction, or love will *conclude* when I make my first million, when I become president of the board, when I get that raise, when I get that promotion, when I achieve that certain status, or when I finally find the relationship of my dreams. Of course, there is nothing wrong with acquiring or achieving any of these things. It's the *why* behind our quest for them that will determine how satisfying they are. If our motivation to prosper is fueled by a sense of personal inadequacy, we will not be satisfied for long with any of the things we accomplish.

In *Lessons in Truth,* H. Emilie Cady writes, "With a restlessness that is pitiful to see, people are ever shifting from one thing to another, always hoping to find rest and satisfaction in some anticipated accomplishment or possession. Men fancy that they want houses and lands, great learning or power. They pursue these things and gain them only to find themselves still restless, still unsatisfied."[1] The reason this is true, the reason the acquisition of things leaves us "restless, still unsatisfied," is that things do not have the power to give us what we can only experience from the depths of our being. *Every desirable state of being that we are trying to derive from our possessions can only permanently be derived from our true Self.*

Many Levels of Conclusionistic Thinking

There are many levels of conclusionistic thinking, and all of us engage in them from time to time. For example, if you have ever been upset by what another person said, if you have ever been depressed by a cloudy day, if you have ever been disappointed that a package didn't arrive, if you have ever given up your peace of mind because you were late for an appointment, you have engaged in a mild form of conclusionistic thinking. You are saying that a desirable internal experience—things like self-approval, peace of mind, self-confidence, happiness—are dependent either on the achievement of certain external things or on conditions being a certain way. These are petty examples to which each of us falls victim, probably many times a day, attitudinal issues that may degrade the quality of the moment but have no significant impact on the overall course and quality of our life. If we are attuned to the role our attitude plays in determining the quality of day we have, we will usually catch ourselves in these negative but temporary reactions to appearances and correct them rather quickly.

Our concern here, especially as it relates to the subject of prosperity, is what might be termed *chronic conclusionism,* whereby we make the *entire* existence and well-being of our personal identity dependent on specific acquisitions and on making conditions unfold in very specific ways. Here, our quest for prosperity is really a quest for the power to manipulate the world into providing us with what we feel we lack as individuals.

In this state of "restlessness" we are always dissatisfied with where we are in life, with who we are as people, and with the conditions that surround us. We fall into the trap of thinking that if we could just make enough money or if we could just move to the right neighborhood, drive the right car, or work for the right company, we would fix everything which is wrong and be happy.

Fleeing the Sad Self

Emerson exemplified the chronic conclusionistic thinker's plight in his essay "Self-Reliance." "At home I dream that at Naples, at Rome, I can be intoxicated with beauty and lose my sadness. I pack my trunk, embrace my friends, embark on the sea and at last wake up in Naples, and there beside me is the stern fact, the sad self, unrelenting, identical, that I fled from."[2]

How successful we are in our quest for a prosperous life will depend on whether our motivation to prosper is based on losing our "sad self" or on discovering and learning to live life from the basis of our true Self. If we are trying, through the process of achievement and material acquisition, to lose our sad self, we will never succeed to our satisfaction. We will always be the same sad self living in the midst of the same dissatisfying life, forever waiting for the next break, the next raise, the next marriage, the next promotion, the next new house, or the next new prosperity book to come into our life and make us feel better. There is nothing necessarily wrong with having or doing any of these things. But if we think any of them can instill qualities in us that can only be evolved from within, we will be disappointed. We will wake up in our "Naples" confronted by the stern fact that, though our external life has changed, *we* are still the same.

Having Equals Being

The conclusionistic thinker operates from a formula that *having equals being.* The reasoning here is that the more we *have* the better off we will *be,* that is, the better we will feel about ourselves. The mistake made in this reasoning is the assumption that having a certain thing will automatically produce in us a certain desirable state of being. But this is not necessarily true. Having a large stack of firewood, for example, is not the same thing as being warm. Our conclusionisticly motivated quest for a more prosperous life can produce enormous stacks of firewood for us. But if that firewood is not ignited with the flame of true Self-discovery, we can literally freeze to death in the middle of it all. This appears to be what is happening with many in our society today. Here we have people whose garages are so full of things they cannot even get their car in. Yet they are still obsessed with the need to acquire more!

Checking Your Motivation to Prosper

One of the most important questions we can ask ourselves in our quest for a more prosperous life is the one I raised at the beginning of this chapter: *"Who is this I whom I am trying to prosper?"* Is the goal in your quest for material achievement and acquisition fueled by the hope of losing your *sad self?* Is your attempt to prosper really an attempt to compensate for a sense of personal inadequacy? Are you trying, through material acquisition, to eliminate a fear of lack? If any of these things are true, it will not matter how much you acquire or accomplish in a material way. You will be dissatisfied with your results because you are not dealing with the true essence of the problem. You may get to your "Naples," but you will always find that you took your inadequate, sad self with you.

A man who attended a prosperity workshop I conducted explained to me that he had grown up in dire poverty. When he reached his mid-teens, he made the decision that he would never be poor again. Over the years he had managed to amass a substantial fortune, and yet, as he explained, he still lived with the nagging fear that he could lose it all and return to his former poverty-stricken condition. The man's motivation to prosper was a fear of lack, which emanated from his inadequate self-image. He had remedied his external condition many times over. But he had never done anything to eliminate the poverty-stricken self-image he was living from. In his mind, poverty was an evil force that could only be overcome with more money. And yet, in spite of the fact that he had acquired an abundance of money, he didn't feel any more prosperous than he did as a child. He woke up in "Naples," only to find he had brought along his sad self—or, in his case, his poor self.

Do You Want to Prosper?

Another very important aspect to consider is that you may have so much invested in your current identity and the lifestyle it produces, that while you say you want to prosper, you may be unconsciously doing everything possible to prevent prosperity from occurring. It might be necessary for you to ask yourself the same question Jesus asked the man who lay for a long time beside the pool known as Beth-zatha and waited to be healed: "Do you want to be healed?"[3]

On the surface this would seem to be a rather ridiculous question for Jesus to ask. Yet the man had been ill for thirty-eight years. One might begin to wonder if healing *was* really what the man wanted. He may have had reasons for remaining in his condition. The responsibilities of being a healthy, walking man may have been greater than he cared to take on. He may have had parents who convinced him he would never amount to anything or an aggressive sibling with whom he could no longer compete. He could have had such low self-esteem that he felt unable to function in a normal social capacity. Maybe this ailment was his way of dealing with his deep sense of inadequacy.

Like most people in my profession, I have run across a number of cases dealing with issues of self-esteem and forgiveness in which ailments that were being treated with drugs responded much better to counseling. The fact that Jesus singled out this man from a "multitude of invalids" gives credibility to speculation that he believed the man's condition was psychologically propagated.

With his question, Jesus was really asking the man if he was ready to give up his current identity as an invalid and begin to live with the new identity of a walking, healthy man. The implications to this question ran very deep. Was the man willing to take on the whole new range of responsibilities that go with the ability to walk? Was he prepared to give up the lifestyle of an invalid? Life by the pool may not have been the best, but it was predictable, he could make a living at it, and it offered him a degree of security. He probably had a great support group and status in that particular community, and if sympathy was one of his requirements, he certainly would have received an abundance of it. Reaching the pool meant placing the survival of his current identity in jeopardy. He had good cause to place himself in a set of circumstances that appeared to make it impossible for him to succeed.

If you have, over the years, read every prosperity book, listened to every tape, attended many prosperity-based lectures and seminars, collected enough prosperity affirmations to cover the entire front of a king-sized refrigerator, yet still have not achieved the level of prosperity you seek, you may have to come to grips with your answer to the question, Do you really want to prosper? The deeper question here, of course, is, Are you prepared to give up the identity that is keeping you from prospering? After so many years of trying and failing to prosper, you may have to accept the fact that your conditions of lack are the inevitable consequence of your self-definition and that if you really want to prosper, you need to die to this self-definition and evolve a new one.

I began smoking cigarettes in my early teen years. At that age, I considered smoking to be an enhancement to my identity as well as a kind of rite of passage into the crowd with which I ran. It was the "cool" thing to do. Over the course of the next several years, this "enhancement" became a two-pack-a-day habit. Many times during this period (about seven years) I tried unsuccessfully to quit smoking.

One day, quite unexpectedly, an interesting thing happened. It was during a particularly transformative period in my life, a time when I was beginning to awaken to the spiritual dimension within myself. I was driving my car and smoking a cigarette when suddenly an image of myself as a person who did not smoke came into my mind. I snuffed out the cigarette and in that instant changed from a person who smoked to a person who did not. Since that moment I have not once been tempted to pick up the habit again.

At the time I was somewhat puzzled with the ease at which I walked away from the smoking habit, especially after having tried and failed so many times before. In retrospect, I understand how it happened. I began smoking out of a sense of inadequacy, the prime motivation behind all conclusionistic thinking. To feel adequate I needed to be part of a crowd. Smoking was one way of accomplishing that. Smoking, then, had become an important extension of my identity. Quitting meant giving up a part of myself. I would, with the best intentions, go through the motions of trying to quit. But until I became willing to give up my inadequate identity, I *had* to remain a smoker. All my efforts to quit were, well, a smoke screen that covered the real issue. If Jesus would have approached me asking, "Do you really want to quit smoking?" my honest answer would have been, "Yes, but if I do I'll have to give up a part of my identity that I still think is important, and I don't think I can do that yet." The moment I became willing to give up the part of my identity that manifested itself as a smoking habit, I was able, like the man by the pool, to take up my pallet and walk.

The way in which you define yourself will determine the nature of the external props you need to play out that definition. The man in the story needed the pool to play out his identity as an invalid. *I* needed a two-pack-a-day smoking habit to compensate for my lack of self-esteem. *You* may need insurmountable obstacles, a job that compromises your integrity, an unfulfilled marriage, poor relationships, poor health, or financial lack to play out the definition you hold of yourself. If you truly want to prosper, if you truly want to relinquish your struggle through life, you have to be sure you're not perpetuating these conditions by living out of a conclusionistic identity that requires them.

As pointed out in a previous chapter, our impulse to prosper is divine in its origin. We want to experience a freer, more expanded life because the universe is seeking to expand through us. However, because many of us have taken on an inadequate self-image, we have transferred this natural impulse to prosper into an acquisitional frenzy that is compensatory, rather than creative, in nature. We are trying to compensate, through material acquisition, for what we feel we lack on an internal level. The result is that our quest for things has become conclusionistic in nature.

If we are to achieve a truly prosperous life, it is *extremely* important for us to understand whether our motivation to do so is fueled by the natural law of infinite expansion or whether our motivation has become compensatory and conclusionistic in nature. If the latter has become the case, the next chapter will give some guidelines on how to remedy this problem. Our objective here is to determine the nature of our motivation to prosper.

A Place to Begin

A good place to begin to understand your motivation to prosper is to ask yourself this question:

In my quest for a more materially prosperous life, am I trying to improve the way I feel about myself through the avenue of material acquisition?

Give this question careful consideration. Are you trying to achieve more self-confidence and security, greater peace of mind, a greater sense of self-respect and self-esteem by making more money, getting a promotion, joining that social club, finding the right relationship, moving to the right neighborhood, or achieving certain status? If so, you are taking the conclusionistic approach to prosperity and the results will be temporary, at best.

Let me point out again that there is nothing wrong with wanting to change the way you feel about yourself and there is nothing wrong with acquiring material things or new positions. The problem lies in the combination of the two, trying to achieve the one through the accomplishment of the other. It is like trying to drive a nail into wood with a pair of pliers. You simply *cannot* change the way you feel about yourself, with any degree of permanence, through the avenue of material acquisition.

All of these internal issues must be addressed head-on, if you are to permanently raise the quality of your experience. You cannot purchase high self-esteem. There is not enough money in the world to eliminate your fear of lack. If you are plagued with the fear of being alone outside a relationship, you will be plagued with that same fear inside a relationship, regardless of how good the relationship is.

When you identify your motivation to prosper, you will then be able to tailor your actions around actually resolving the real issues. You will find that you don't have to get to Beth-zatha to take up your pallet and walk. You don't have to go to Naples to lose your sad self. You can begin right where you are. Then, when you do begin to lose your sad self, you can go to Naples and have a wonderful time!

Summary

1. Am I trying to prosper the true spiritual being which I am or am I trying to prosper the limited self-image which I think I need to be?

2. Am I a conclusionistic thinker? Do I think I will finally reach a state of happiness and satisfaction through some form of external accomplishment?

3. Am I trying to get to a specific "Naples" so I can lose my *sad self*? Am I operating from the formula that *having equals being*?

4. If I have read all the prosperity books and applied all the prosperity techniques with little success, then I must ask myself this question: Do I really want to prosper, or am I more interested in protecting a weak self-image? The moment I get sincere about prospering as the spiritual being that I am is the moment I will begin to prosper.

Chapter 6

The Evolutionistic Approach

Understanding Evolution

We can think of the achievement of a prosperous life through Self-discovery in much the same way we would think of achieving balance when riding a bicycle to the corner market to buy a loaf of bread. Achieving balance on your bicycle is important, but it's not your objective. Your objective is to purchase a loaf of bread. Balance is the by-product of your movement toward your greater objective. In the same way, the condition of material prosperity, like balance, is the natural by-product of your higher objective of Self-discovery.

Self-discovery, according to Charles Fillmore, is a process of unfolding "that which God involved in man in the beginning."[1] The true Self, a perfect expression of God, is already whole, complete. Once we begin to understand the nature of this Self—synonymous with the "kingdom" Jesus spoke of—we begin to understand that the qualities we are looking for in our material acquisitions already exist within us.

We may seek to acquire more money, for example, because we believe it will give us greater freedom. The true Self already exists in an absolute state of freedom. The reason we do not feel free is because we have taken on a lesser identity. We have gotten away from our true Self. The practice of meditation reveals that the closer we get to this Self, the more freedom we experience. The more freedom we experience by living from the true Self, the more we tend to attract into our lives the material symbols like money and conditions that represent freedom. The secret of living a prosperous life, as Jesus said, is to seek first the inner "kingdom," the true Self, and everything that you need in a material way will be naturally attracted to you. I will deal extensively with this phenomenon of attraction in the following chapter, "Changing Your Circumstantial Tendencies."

The Evolutionistic Approach

Our evolutionary process, then, involves a major shift in the way we think about prosperity. We gradually move from the conclusionistic belief that things hold the power to make us happy to what I call the *evolutionistic* approach. This approach to prosperity says that the quality of experience we are really seeking in life must first be *evolved* from within. Remember that the conclusionistic formula, *having equals being,* says the more you *have* the happier you should *be.* The evolutionistic formula is exactly the opposite. It says that *being equals having.* Discover and live from your natural state of happiness. Be happy, and you will *have* a happy life.

The quality of experience we are trying to derive from our material possessions already exists within the realm of our true Self. That we desire this quality of experience in the first place is evidence that the true Self is naturally evolving, attempting to externalize through us that which is already "involved" at the deepest level of our being. The author of the book of Revelation gave voice to this Self when he wrote, "Behold, I stand at the door and knock"[2] Our true Self is "standing" at the door of our consciousness, continually asserting its presence as the desire for a more abundant life.

The Realm of Symbols

The material realm is a realm of *symbols.* Everything we seek, in a material way, represents our search for some aspect of a deeper reality. Money is, among other things, a symbol of *freedom, security,* and *power.* The conclusionistic thinker reasons that if he or she has enough money, the deeper experiences of freedom, security, and power will follow naturally. The evolutionistic thinker, on the other hand, realizes that freedom, security, and power are qualities of the true Self which must first be expressed from within if they are to be experienced with any degree of permanency. As we evolve these qualities from within, we begin to attract the external symbols as well.

For example, people who are free from egotistical hang-ups and who are secure in their identities and natural presence of power will be much more successful in life than people who are hampered by their fears, insecure about who they are, and dependent on other people and things for their power. If you were an employer and two people who displayed these different characteristics walked into your office asking for an important position, which one would you hire? Would you want the one who expresses self-confidence or the one who obviously needs an emotional baby-sitter?

If it is true, that everything we seek in a material way represents our search for some aspect of a deeper reality, then the secret of success lies in identifying this deeper reality and evolving it through our consciousness. Remember, the quality of experience we are trying to derive from our material possessions already exists within the realm of our true Self. The essence of what we are seeking through material acquisition is always within our reach. It is only a matter of learning how to bring it to the surface of our being.

Go to Your Inner Place of Peace

Let's look at a practical example of how this might work in everyday life. Your teenage child is late coming home from a school dance, and this has you worried. You are robbed of your peace of mind. From a conclusionistic point of view, you reason that when your child comes home, your peace of mind will be restored. In other words, you are making your ability to experience peace of mind dependent on knowing where your child is. In reality, however, your true Self is *always* in a state of peace and the experience of peace is always accessible to you. Not knowing your child's whereabouts does not take this away. You have allowed only the more surface level of your mind to be disturbed by the absence of your child. It is possible for you to experience a deep sense of peace even though your child is not home. You can take time to release your emotional disturbance, go deeper within yourself to your inner place of peace, and begin to have a peaceful experience. This is the evolutionistic approach to attaining peace. You recognize that peace is a quality which, as Fillmore said, has been involved in you from the beginning. You make the choice to go into that peace and evolve it out through your consciousness.

Does this evolutionary approach bring your child home any faster? Not necessarily. But it does provide you with the experience you are trying to derive by getting your child home. It will give you peace of mind. Isn't this your main objective? As a parent of two children, now in their late teens, I know what it is to not know where my children are. I also know that if my reaction to not knowing where they are is one of worry and fear, then I have a miserable experience while I wait for them to come home. It didn't take long to discover that my having a miserable experience while I waited never brought them home any faster. It also didn't take long to discover that if my teenage children were in charge of my peace of mind, I might as well forget having any for the next few years!

I once received a phone call from a frantic mother whose daughter, after having threatened suicide, had run away from home. When I arrived at the parents' house, I was surprised to see they were in their mid-seventies. I was even more surprised to discover that the daughter was forty-two years old! It seems that this little game had been going on for years. Both parents had put their daughter in complete charge of their peace of mind. Whenever the daughter wanted a display of "affection," she would pull this disappearing act. When it was discovered that the daughter was fine, the mother breathed a great sigh of relief and said, "I swear that girl's going to be the death of me!" It was obvious to me, however, that if the mother died of a stroke or heart failure because of the manipulative ploys of her daughter, then her death would be, in actuality, a kind of suicide.

We have been talking about peace of mind with this illustration. But as I said earlier, *everything* we are trying to achieve through material acquisition has a spiritual counterpart that already exists as an integral aspect of our true Self. The desire for money is a desire for freedom, power, and security. The desire for an intimate relationship might be a desire for love or self-acceptance. The desire for your right work is a desire for creative Self-expression. Freedom, power, security, love, self-acceptance, and the ability to creatively express yourself are all accessible to you, right now, in this very moment, because these qualities are an integral aspect of your true Self.

Four Steps in the Evolutionistic Approach

There are four basic steps involved in the evolutionistic approach to living a more prosperous life. They are as follows:

1. Identify the inner quality or state of being you wish to experience.

2. Realize this quality is already an integral element of your true Self.

3. Begin to evolve this quality from within your-self until it becomes a state of being.

4. Know this state of being will draw to you the external symbol or symbols that best repre-sent it.

Let's take a closer look at each of these steps.

1. *Identify the inner quality or state of being you wish to experience.*

When operating from the conclusionistic point of view, we rarely consider this vital step. To use the above example, we expend most of our energy trying to find out where our child is instead of ask-ing ourselves what it is we are trying to get from doing so. What we are after, in this case, is peace of mind. Behind every desire to acquire something on the material level, is really a desire to change the way we feel. To discover what it is we want to feel, we can think of the thing we desire, then simply ask ourselves this question: *What feeling or feel-ings do I want the accomplishment of this thing to in-still in me?*

Here are some examples of answers to this ques-tion that have come from people who attended pros-perity classes I have taught.

One man said: "I want this promotion because I feel so powerless on the job. Everyone's always telling me what to do, and I think I know more about the company than they do." This man believed a promotion would instill in him a feeling of *power.*

A woman said, "I want to win the lottery so I can do whatever I want." She believed that winning the lottery would instill in her a feeling of *freedom.*

A man said, "I'd like to make enough money so I wouldn't have to worry about anything." He believed that making money would instill in him feelings of *security* and *freedom.*

A young woman said, "I want to get married and have a family because that would be so fulfilling." She believed that getting married and having a family would instill in her feelings of *completeness.*

Another woman said, "I want a good relationship because I want the feeling that someone really loves me." This woman believed that having a good relationship would instill in her the feelings of *security, love,* and perhaps *self-acceptance.*

The feeling you want to achieve is your real objective. It is, to use our earlier example, your loaf of bread. Clearly and carefully define the feeling or feelings you wish to experience, then write them down. When you are satisfied that you have defined what it is you are after, go on to the next step.

2. *Realize this quality is already an integral element of your true Self.*

The feeling you want to experience is now completely accessible to you. Your desire to experience it, remember, is your real Self pushing forth this aspect of Itself into your conscious mind. Your ability to achieve this feeling is not dependent on having the thing you think will bring it. Separate your true goal from the particular means you have designated as being the only way that you can experience what you want.

3. *Begin to evolve this quality from within yourself until it becomes a state of being.*

Allow yourself to feel the feeling you desire. Feel powerful. Feel secure. Feel peaceful. Feel love. Feel complete self-acceptance. Feel the feeling you think this thing will instill in you. Practice this feeling in quiet times and practice it throughout your busy day. Work with it until you can call it up at will. Continue to call it up until it becomes a dominant element of your consciousness. When events transpire that say you should have lesser feelings, release them as quickly as possible. Release this false belief that says the feeling you desire is dependent on things going a certain way. You are the one who makes the choice about how you feel. Practice harboring only those feelings you desire to experience.

4. *Know this state of being will draw to you the external symbol or symbols that best represent it.*

Being equals having. As you become in consciousness the person you really are, your whole life will begin to reflect it. If the parents of the 42-year-old woman would stop feeding into her game, do you think she would continue it? Their external experience would improve because they would take charge of their feelings of peace. If the man who felt powerless on the job would allow himself to begin to feel powerful, he would gradually begin to make new choices that would eventually set up a whole new set of circumstances for him. Acting on this feeling may take him to the top of the corporate ladder, or it may take him in a completely new direction. If the woman who wanted to win the lottery began to allow herself to experience feelings of absolute freedom right in the midst of her current life, she, too, would begin to make a whole new set of choices that would have the effect of opening doors she thought were locked.

Day after day the strength of your feeling will grow and you will notice subtle and not-so-subtle changes. Your attitude will change. Your expectation of good will increase. Your confidence will build. You will notice that external conditions affect you less. You will find yourself making decisions and new choices based on this emerging state of being. You will become acutely aware of self-defeating thought patterns and actions, and begin to release them. In short, you will notice more and more that your new state of being is impacting your lifestyle. Before you know it, you will not only *be* the person you desire, you will *have* the things and conditions that are equivalent to the person you have become. You and I are not designed to be victims of circumstance. We are designed to live life to its fullest. The way to do so is always within our reach. *Being equals having!*

Summary

1. The attainment of material prosperity is not my objective, but is rather the natural by-product of my Self-discovery and Self-expression.

2. Everything I am trying to achieve through material acquisition has a spiritual counterpart that already exists as an integral aspect of my true Self.

3. My prosperity comes from evolving, from within myself, that which God involved in me from the beginning.

Chapter 7

Changing Your Circumstantial Tendencies

Your Life Is No Accident

The overall quality of our life does not unfold the way it does by chance. There is a direct correlation between what we believe about ourselves and the direction our life takes. If we are to successfully create the life we intuitively know is possible for us, it is vital we understand how circumstances that are unique to us are created and sustained.

A Point of Clarification

Before embarking upon this subject, I want to make one thing clear. When I refer to circumstances, I am not speaking so much of individual events as I am the overall direction your life is moving. I am not interested in trying to help you understand why every single thing happens in your life the way it does. I am only interested in helping you understand why you keep experiencing similar outcomes in whatever you undertake, a phenomenon that I will be referring to as *circumstantial tendencies*. Why do some keep having failed relationships, for example, while others have no trouble at all? Why can't some hold a steady job,while others progress steadily over the years through their careers? Why do some fail at business ventures, while others succeed at everything they do? Why do some always seem to fall just short of accomplishing their objectives, while others always seem to get what they want?

All of us have things happen in our lives that are difficult, if not impossible, to explain to our satisfaction. In these cases I believe it is more important to understand our particular reaction to the circumstance than it is to understand the origin of the circumstance itself. Changing tendencies in circumstances, not explaining the origin of individual circumstances, is what this chapter is about.

To many, the realm of circumstance and their influence upon it remains a mystery. Evolutionary thinkers understand, however, that both the direction and the quality of their circumstantial tendencies are governed primarily by the *self-image* they carry. The unique way our individual life unfolds has *everything* to do with the way we see ourselves. Why? Because the way we see ourselves has a direct influence on what we believe about everything, from our personal capabilities, to our relationship to the world, to our place in the universe in general. The self-image affects our entire *belief system*. Our belief system, in turn, is the primary influence on the *decisions* we make. And the decisions we make determine our *actions,* the most visible influence on our circumstantial tendencies.

Not Just Self-Image Psychology

As discussed in the previous chapter, the evolutionary approach is to first evolve from within the state of being that we wish to experience. In so doing, we know that improved circumstantial tendencies will follow. *Being equals having.* In this evolutionary process, we are actually bringing forth a new, spiritually based self-image. As your self-image changes, your belief system changes, the decisions you make are different, and the actions you take will create a whole new set of circumstances for you.

If it sounds as if I am talking about little more than an exercise in self-image psychology here, it is important to remember that we are, at least in part, psychological beings. It is at the psychological level that we have the most influence on our circumstantial tendencies. It is a well-established fact that what we *believe to be true* has more influence on the quality of our circumstances than Truth itself. The objective of our spiritual evolution, of course, is to change that. Our spiritual evolution is a process of re-establishing our psychological identity, our self-image, upon the foundation of our true, spiritual Self. Eventually our self-image will become, in biblical terms, that *image and likeness of God* which we are created to be.

A Biblical Example

As it so often does, the Bible offers a good illustration of the importance of self-image and the role it plays in determining how our circumstances unfold. The story is found in the thirteenth chapter of the book of Numbers.

After having wandered in the wilderness for forty years, Moses brought the nation of Israel to the border of the land the Lord had promised Abraham a few generations before. Moses, desiring to measure the strength and numbers of the native occupants of this land, sent in twelve spies on an intelligence-gathering mission. Upon their return, the twelve were summoned to give an assessment of their observations. All twelve agreed that it was indeed a land of abundance, a land "flowing with milk and honey."[1] What they did not agree on, however, was whether or not Israel possessed the strength to overcome the inhabitants. The majority of spies, eleven to be exact, reported that "the people who dwell in the land are strong, and the cities are fortified and very large." Their conclusion? "We are not able to go up against the people; for they are stronger than we."

There was one spy, Caleb, who did not reach the same conclusion as the other eleven. His advice to Israel was this: "Let us go up at once, and occupy it; for we are well able to overcome it."[2]

How could it be that Caleb and his eleven companions could see the same people but evaluate them in two completely different ways? The answer is simple. These conflicting evaluations were not based on the actual people they saw. Their evaluations were based on *how they saw themselves*. This interesting fact is revealed in the report of the eleven when they said, "We seemed to ourselves like grasshoppers, and so we seemed to them."[3]

Naturally, if you see yourself as a "grasshopper," it is going to affect the way you create your circumstances. First of all, it will affect what you *believe* you can and cannot do. These beliefs will influence the *decisions* you make, your decisions will determine your *actions,* and your actions will influence the way your circumstances unfold.

Because they saw themselves as grasshoppers, the eleven did not believe they could overcome the inhabitants of the land. They made the decision to recommend to Moses and the assembly that they take no action against these inhabitants. If the assembly had accepted their recommendation, Israel would not have occupied their land of promise. The circumstances of an entire nation would have been adversely affected by the grasshopper self-image of these eleven spies.

Caleb, on the other hand, apparently did not see himself as a grasshopper. He saw himself as a warrior for the Lord who was simply accepting the land the Lord had promised Israel through Abraham years before. This self-image gave him quite a different perspective of the situation. It caused him to believe Israel, through the strength of the Lord's promise, could overcome these inhabitants. Caleb's recommended action was that they proceed. If they had, they may have avoided the necessity of wandering forty years in the wilderness.

Two Types of Self-Image

The conclusionistic thinker and the evolutionistic thinker see the world from two completely different types of self-images. The conclusionistic thinker operates from a self-image that is based on a strong sense of personal inadequacy. Conclusionistic thinkers draw most of their identity, their power, and much of their meaning for living from other people, careers, personal appearance, size of their bank account, their social standing, and so on. They measure their identities and their capabilities using an inventory of external assets.

Evolutionistic thinkers, on the other hand, live more *centered* lives, drawing their identity, power, and meaning for living from within themselves. They know they are eternally connected to their unlimited Source, and they measure their identities and their capabilities not by what they have, but by who they are spiritually.

The eleven spies were conclusionistic thinkers. Caleb was an evolutionistic thinker. The eleven, who were operating from a strong sense of personal inadequacy, a "grasshopper" self-image, evaluated the problem from the basis of their inventory of external assets. Since their inventory appeared to be lacking—they were physically smaller and were probably outnumbered—they assumed they would be unable to defeat these inhabitants.

Caleb probably took these obvious facts into account, but they did not deter his recommendation to move forward. The evolutionistic thinker does not have to have all the answers to apparent problems before he or she makes a decision. Evolutionistic thinkers' decisions are not based on appearances. They are based on their unlimited spiritual capacity. They know that solutions to each problem which arises will *evolve* as they are needed.

The important point of the story is this: Had the

Israelites made their decision based on Caleb's opinion they would not have had to wander in the wilderness. But since they made their decision based on the opinion of the eleven, their circumstances unfolded in quite a different way. The difference can be traced back to the quality of a particular type of self-image.

The better we understand this fact, the less likely we are to call ourselves victims of circumstance and the more likely we are to take charge of our own destiny. If you measure what you can do in life by what you have in your personal inventory of external assets, you may never experience the life of your dreams. Either you will spend your most productive years building up your inventory, or your inventory will never be quite big enough to instill in you the confidence to launch your campaign. You can, of course, blame circumstances for your failure, and you'll probably get plenty of sympathy. Remember, Caleb was the only one of the twelve who voted to go forward. The eleven, I'm sure, felt perfectly comfortable with their decision, just out of sheer numbers. If eleven out of twelve people figure it can't be done, then it probably can't be done. But aren't we glad there have been at least a few evolutionistic thinkers through the ages who disagree with this type of conclusionistic logic!

Changing our circumstantial tendencies is a

process that involves a scrutinizing awareness of the four areas we have talked about. We need to be aware of the type of *self-image* from which we are living, whether it is conclusionistic or evolutionistic in nature. We need to be aware of the kinds of *beliefs* we hold about ourselves in relation to the particular issues with which we are dealing. We need to understand how these beliefs are affecting the *decisions* we make. And we need to be aware of our *actions* as we interact with the external world. Above all, once we know what it is about ourselves that we need to change, we must actually take the necessary steps to change it. It is important to remember that *nothing about our circumstantial tendencies will change until we change the way we see ourselves.* This is a responsibility we have to be willing to accept if we are to create the life we know we can have.

A Personal Testimony

At the time I began to reignite my musical career, a friend suggested that I do a concert for the people of Evergreen, Colorado, based on my album *One World.* This would be a full-band production, complete with backup singers. The primary objective of the concert would be to build community awareness of our church. My music, he thought, would be an excellent way to get our Unity message out without appearing to proselytize. While I agreed with the concept, I had many reservations about such an undertaking.

Because it had been many years since I had last performed in a live situation with a band, the "performer" aspect of my self-image had become very weak and grasshopper-like. When I took an inventory of my external assets, I found there were not many. I didn't have the band or singers necessary to reproduce the *One World* music. We didn't have the money to produce the event. That would have to come in through ticket sales, which meant we would need to spend substantial amounts for advertising, location, printing, and so on, without knowing if expenses would be covered in the end. The most important thing I was lacking was self-confidence. What I did have in my inventory of assets was a strong group of people who had a lot more confidence in me than I had in myself at that moment.

The problem with others providing your self-confidence is that you only have it when they are around. With each planning meeting, I would feel a new flush of confidence. But when I was alone, the doubts would creep in. People can encourage us, but the confidence we need to do the things we need to do, to really go the distance, can only come from within us.

We want a certain quality of life. I wanted to perform musically in exactly the kind of situation we were setting up. So why was I trying to find every reason not to do it when the opportunity finally arose? Because I was afraid. I was looking at the world through the eyes of a grasshopper. That, in itself, is not what keeps us from moving into the life we desire. Anytime you do something new, anytime you put yourself in a place you've never been before, your "grasshopper" self is going to arise and try to convince you to turn back. It's when you actually turn back that your life remains the same. At some point we must set our fears aside and force ourselves to take the next step. And this is the point I finally reached.

I knew I could no longer afford to be the victim of my own self-doubt. I finally became internally solidified, pulling out every stop that was keeping me from moving forward. I evolved new strength and self-confidence, and I totally committed myself to the success of this event. In short, all the things I feared dissolved as we moved forward. The result was that the concert was a complete success.

I realize this story is not based on an earthshaking, life-or-death struggle for survival. But it is the kind of story that makes up most of what our life is. We want a certain quality of circumstances, but we deny ourselves this quality when, through our fears and lack of self-confidence, we make choices that do not allow these circumstances to unfold. My lack of self-confidence caused me to make decisions and take actions that would actually frustrate the manifestation of something I really wanted. Here I was at the border of my own "promised land," only to find myself on the verge of turning away. If being a concert musician was one thing I wanted to do in my life, then at some point I had to make the decision to push past every fear that had kept me from doing it in the first place.

Are you sitting at the border of some promised land, unable to enter? How do you see yourself in this situation? Do you see yourself as a grasshopper? Do you feel small in comparison to the task ahead? What do you believe must happen before you can move into this promised land? I will tell you what must happen. You must change your self-image. You must begin to draw your strength and confidence from the depths of your true Self. You must agree to move forward from this basis. With this agreement comes a natural change in what you believe you can or cannot do. You will make new decisions and take new actions that will produce for you the kinds of circumstances you have always desired.

Summary

1. The creation of my circumstantial tendencies is not a mystery to me. They result from a com-

bination of my *self-image,* my *belief system,* the *decisions* I make, and the *actions* I take.

2. I can change my circumstantial tendencies by changing the way I see myself.

3. I can ask myself, in every situation, whether I am seeing myself as a grasshopper or as an unlimited expression of God. I can choose to see myself as an unlimited expression of God.

Chapter 8

Meeting the Dynamics of Challenge

Confrontation Is Inevitable

It is important to realize that every new enterprise, every decision you make to pursue your passion is going to evoke some level of confrontation between the stronger and the weaker elements of your self-image. You will set your goals based on your strengths, your talents, your interests, and your dreams. In the process of manifesting them, however, you will encounter challenges that will summon all your weaknesses as well. Self-doubt, fear of failure, feelings of lack, impatience, anger, lethargy, and indifference will all creep in at the most inappropriate times. Like Job, you may find yourself saying, "The thing that I fear comes upon me, and what I dread befalls me."[1] Many worthy undertakings have been brought to a grinding halt by these unwelcome thieves of our creative energy.

We need not be taken by surprise when this seemingly negative side of our consciousness arises.

While it may not always be comfortable or convenient, the arousal of these stifling elements is both inevitable and necessary. They arise from that limited aspect of our identity which is crying out to be redefined from the basis of our true Self. Because of the discomfort or even pain involved in dealing with them, the temptation is to suppress these unwanted elements. But unless the things we fear most do come upon us, unless they are brought into the full light of our awareness, we will never be able to trace them back to their sources and permanently release the negative influence they have on our circumstantial tendencies.

What Is a Challenge?

Every challenge holds something of value for us. It is our responsibility to find out what that "something" is, and it is our responsibility to do what is necessary to benefit from the information we glean. A good place to begin is to understand what a challenge is.

Roughly defined, a challenge is any situation that appears to require more from us than it appears we have in our inventory of assets. We may think that we need more faith, wisdom, courage, self-confidence, love, understanding, or additional material resources such as money. We respond to challenges from either a conclusionistic or evolutionistic mode of thinking.

In the conclusionistic mode, we evaluate the situation by first checking our inventory of external assets to see if we have enough to overpower the challenge. If our inventory is inadequate to meet the challenge, we are conditioned by our conclusionistic thinking to react negatively. All our inadequacies are brought to the surface in the form of fear, self-doubt, resentment, feelings of being victimized, the belief that the accomplishment of our dream was too good to be true, and so on. Because we are measuring the challenge according to what we have in our inventory of external assets, the challenge becomes a problem that appears to be beyond our capacity to handle.

In our evolutionary thinking mode, we will handle the same challenge in a completely different way. We will still draw from our inventory of external assets, but we will not restrict ourselves by them. We will not allow our thinking or our actions to be limited by what we have or do not have, in an external way. We know our greatest asset is our ability to go within ourselves to that unlimited reservoir of wisdom, strength, courage, and inspiration. Our confidence is based, not on what we *have,* but on who we *are,* in truth.

Moments in Gethsemane

Yes, there will be moments when, even in our evolutionistic mode of thinking, we will still waver.
There will be many moments when fear and self-
doubt will creep in. Like Jesus, we will have our
nights in Gethsemane when we will pray that this
"cup" be removed from our experience, that an easier way than the one which apparently lies ahead of
us be opened. But we know, deep in our heart of
hearts, that within us is the potential to evolve any
state of being necessary for us to rise to the occa-
sion. We may not always see the way immediately,
but we are forever optimistic that there *is* a way and
that the way will become clear to us as we agree to
continue to move forward. We realize that sometimes the bridge to our greater good does not ap-
pear until we step out, beyond our fears, into the
abyss that lies ahead. Then we find support in ways
we could not imagine while we sat contemplating
that apparently impassable chasm.

A Land Purchase

When Beth and I moved to Evergreen, our church
was meeting in a small rented facility. It was obvious
that we would soon outgrow this building and that
something would have to be done. There was talk

about buying land and building a church, but having slipped into my conclusionistic mode of thinking, I viewed our inventory of assets and was hard-pressed to think we could do that. After all, land in Colorado is expensive. We had no money in the bank and were just meeting expenses. In addition, we were only averaging about forty people on a Sunday.

A realtor friend in our church told me of a tract of nearly sixteen acres that had been on the market for quite some time. She suggested that the board and I take a look at it, so we did. The place was indeed beautiful, but it also had a price tag of $170,000, far too much for a church the size of ours. Again, looking at our inventory of assets, I figured it would be between five and seven years before we could even think of purchasing something like that. As the months passed, other options for our church building were explored, but none of them showed any promise. The land continued to be on the market.

Somewhere in this process, something in me clicked and I suddenly shifted into my evolutionistic mode of thinking. I became inspired by the prospects of purchasing the land and moving forward with a building project. My board, which was already in its evolutionistic mode of thinking from hiring me in the first place, readily agreed to go for it. We decided to propose to our congregation that we make an offer on the land. The congregation enthusiastically agreed. In less than two months, that small group of people came forth with $96,000! We were then able to borrow an additional $50,000 (the price had dropped in the meantime) to purchase the land for our future church home.

Had I allowed the conclusionistic thinker in me to remain in charge, our church would not now be the proud owner of a beautiful mountain meadow, complete with its own herd of wild elk and a wonderful view of the snowcapped Rockies. We would still be working toward increasing our inventory of external assets and dreaming about it all. Of course, purchasing the land is only the first phase of our journey of building the church. But we are moving forward in the confidence that with each unique set of challenges which is presented along the way, a unique set of solutions will also present itself. This is the nature of the evolutionary process.

Beyond Our External Assets

We need to bear in mind that, from both spiritual and material points of view, we prosper in life only to the extent that we become willing to move, in thought and in action, beyond the protective realm of our inventory of external assets. This means, of course, that if our identity, status, courage, and strength are dependent on what we have in this inventory, there will be times when we feel completely vulnerable to the challenges we encounter. It is what we do in these periods of vulnerability that determines how successful, satisfying, and prosperous our life becomes. If we react in fear, doing everything within our power to protect our own sense of inadequacy, we will benefit little by the challenge. If we work toward identifying and releasing those aspects of our identity that would have us turn away in fear and self-doubt from the quality of experience we really want, the challenge will stimulate new growth in us. We will, in essence, redefine ourselves through the process of meeting the challenge. We begin to understand that the challenges we experience in life provide us with a necessary refining process. They help us to get in touch with the growth-inhibiting beliefs we carry about ourselves and our world.

The Death of Our Weaker Elements

When salmon begin their journey upstream to spawn, they are forced to confront and overcome many obstacles. Many actually die before they reach their destinations. Because only the strongest survive the ordeal, scientists believe this is nature's way of assuring that the salmon will pass on only the strongest genes.

In a similar way, a part of us, those conclusionistic elements of our identity, must "die" so that the stronger aspects of our true Self may emerge. The part of us which is attached to and governed by limited appearances must give way to the greater, eternally stable part which knows no limitation. And often we do not know this limiting aspect of ourselves until we are confronted with conditions that overpower it.

It isn't long after one moves to Colorado that the residents begin asking the inevitable question: "Have you been skiing yet?" To a Missouri flatlander like me, this question is loaded with intimidating ramifications. There was simply nothing in my inventory of external assets that would make me want to strap a pair of seven-foot boards to my feet and slide down a mountain while attempting to remain standing. Of course, I hadn't been skiing yet, and as far as I was concerned, I didn't need to learn until I was reincarnated as the child of a family who lived in the Alps.

The day came, however, when my friend Brian, a former ski instructor, informed me that we were going skiing. One of the drawbacks of being a Unity minister, I jokingly assert, is that Sunday after Sunday you stand up in front of people and tell them that they can do whatever they set their minds to and that they should accept life's challenges in order to stimulate new growth and prosperity. Then one of

your members comes up to you and presents *you*
with a challenge that is nothing short of terrifying.
You want to set a good example, but you also want to
remain alive to present next Sunday's lesson.

On the slopes, the first thing Brian did was teach
me how to fall. I caught on to that quickly. Getting up,
however, was a bit more challenging. In a short time
I was wedging, or snowplowing, my way down the
"bunny" hill, gradually gaining confidence with each
new phase of the learning process. The second time
out, he took me to Vail. Here he guided me through
the gentler slopes, where I could practice my newly
acquired techniques in a relatively safe environment.
Not wanting to hold him back from enjoying his day
at Vail, I encouraged him to go off and ski where he
wanted, assuring him I would be fine practicing by
myself. Shortly after he left, however, I found myself
completely lost and disoriented. The map I held in
my hands suddenly became a map from a different
ski resort. Everything was different. To top it off, the
thing I had feared most had come upon me, or vice
versa. Because I had made several wrong turns, I
suddenly found myself staring down a slope that
looked like a cliff, and I saw no way out other than to
go straight down. You simply cannot ski back uphill
with a downhill pair of skis. This was no case of making a mountain out of a molehill. This really was a
mountain, and somehow I had to get off it!

Many falls and a seeming eternity later, I made it to the bottom—amazingly, with everything but my pride intact. Pride is not something you can maintain as you tumble down a mountain crying out for your mother. Needless to say, at that moment I was ready to hang up my skis.

I did not hang them up, however, but continued over the weeks to meet this challenge of learning to ski. At the end of the season, Brian and I returned to Vail, where I was determined to confront my fears and redefine the negative memories that surrounded that earlier experience. I found I could ski those same slopes with little difficulty. In fact, I didn't even realize they were the same slopes until Brian pointed it out. It all looked so different, now that I had evolved as somewhat of a skier.

Meeting the challenges involved in learning how to ski has evolved a whole new dimension in me. Where did this "skier" aspect of my identity come from? It had lain hidden beneath my fears and inhibitions. To pull it out, I had had to reach into myself, push past my fears, and go for it. It was awkward, humiliating, and frightening before it was fun. Now a whole new dimension in my external life has opened, because I have evolved a new identity, a new set of beliefs about myself as a skier, a new set of decisions (I now own my own ski equipment), and a new set of actions. This is exactly how every new dimension in our life opens up.

Different Results Mean Different Actions

I often remind people (especially myself) that if you want different results in your life, you must stop doing the same things. There are many who do not like their lives the way they are. Every day they get up and go through the same routines, complaining about them the whole time but doing little or nothing different to change them. Yet when something *does* come along to change them, usually a crisis of some sort, they work as quickly as possible to get everything back into the old, predictable routines.

Creating a life of prosperity is all about change, and particularly about changing ourselves. We must agree to move from a lesser, more restricted state of being to a greater, freer state of being. Because of the discomforts involved in change, we often avoid it as long as we possibly can. To many, the driving force behind their desire to prosper is really a desire to avoid having to change themselves, exactly the opposite of what it should be. Their attempts to prosper can often be for the purpose of protecting a weakness, instead of evolving a strength. They reason that if they can figure out a way to finance their current limited identity and the lifestyle it entails, they can avoid the pain of having to scrutinize it.

A woman called once asking me if there were any special affirmations that could help her win the lottery. In our conversation, she told me that her husband had died years ago and that the insurance money he left her was about to run out. Though she was relatively young, she felt that going out and getting work was beneath her dignity, that the lifestyle she had grown accustomed to simply would not permit it. Eventually she revealed that she was afraid to get a job, that there was nothing she could do, because she never had had to work before. I suggested that it would probably take her less time to learn a skill than it would to win the lottery and that the experience of working might arouse interests in her she didn't know she had. In time she followed this suggestion, taking a job using her word processing skills. Eventually she went into her own business and became more excited about her life than she had been in years. She literally became a different person in the process.

What It Takes

It takes courage to go out of our way to face the fears that our challenges stir in us. It takes a genuine commitment to our spiritual evolution to have the presence of mind, right in the middle of the challenge, to realize that the person who is quaking amidst this great turmoil is not the person we really are. It often takes prolonged effort to remember that we were not given a spirit of fear, but rather a Spirit that is strong with the strength of an underlying, eternal reality that knows no limitation, no weakness, no fear. It takes faith to let go of our familiar reference points and move into areas that extend beyond what we can safely manage with our inventory of assets.

Every challenge with which you are confronted is providing you the opportunity to identify and eliminate your conclusionistic patterns of thought and behavior. In every single one, you are putting more faith in your external inventory of assets, or lack of them, than you are in your ability to evolve the state of being you desire. In so doing, you are limiting the quality of your state of being to an unnecessarily undesirable level. In shifting to the evolutionistic approach of *being equals having,* you can begin now to change it and to prosper through every challenge you encounter.

Summary

1. I realize that every new enterprise will evoke some level of confrontation between the stronger

and weaker elements of my self-image. The things I fear most will come upon me.

2. I will not be surprised or daunted by this fact, but will welcome the opportunity to release these weaker elements.

3. I will evaluate every challenge from the standpoint of my limitless Self. I will not allow my progress to be halted by limiting appearances.

4. I am willing to get new results by doing different things. I do not allow my actions to become inhibited by my fear of change, but welcome the new growth opportunities change brings.

Chapter 9

Setting Your Goal and Letting Go

Happiness Is Your Natural State

The conclusionistic model assumes it is a lack of something that stands between us and our happiness. We must, according to the logic of this model, strive to acquire that thing if we are to be happy. Contrary to this logic, however, happiness is the natural state of our true Self. The more aware we are of our true Self, the happier we become. The condition of unhappiness is really nothing more than the result of trying to replace an unawakened aspect of ourselves with some kind of artificial substitute. This substitute can come in many forms: a particular role, a career position, a relationship, money, and, in fact, any external thing from which we are attempting to derive our security, our power, our peace of mind, or our identity. What makes us unhappy is that we cling to things which are less than we are at the deepest level of our being.

The evolutionistic model, on the other hand, begins with the assumption that the true Self is complete, that the state of happiness is not induced through the acquisition of external things, but is, rather, evolved from within.

Because happiness is our natural state of being, the only way to actually achieve it is through *letting go* of that which makes us unhappy. This does not mean that we must divest ourselves of the various roles we play or the things we possess. We are to reach the realization that the sense of identity and personal power we are trying to derive from these roles can only be unfolded from the depths of our being. As a helium balloon naturally rises when it is released, so our state of being rises to its natural state of happiness when we release the weight of the conclusionistic belief that something external must be added to us if we are to be complete.

The Paradox of Goal Setting and Letting Go

This concept of letting go seems to stand in direct conflict with goal-setting. As a result, many people, in the name of evolving higher spiritual ideals, abandon goal setting as a manipulative exercise of the personal will. This is unfortunate, for it is through the activity of setting goals that we can consciously and positively affect our circumstantial tendencies.

It is not the practice of following our own will, in

the very truest sense of the word, that gets us into trouble. It is using our will to avoid the discomforts of change and transition that often accompany the inner work needed which gets us into trouble. You desire freedom, for example, and you decide that making more money will give it to you. So you exercise your will to create circumstances whereby you will make more money. The problem, of course, is that money cannot instill in you the kind of freedom you deeply crave. Your state of *having* will not raise your state of *being*. What is really needed is some internal housecleaning. There is a need to release your fear of lack, your belief in limited appearances, and, above all, your belief that something external can create in you the free state of being you desire. The desire for freedom is, indeed, spiritually born. But the exercise of your will to demonstrate freedom is, in this case, limited in its scope. Failure to acquire the desired state of freedom through the accumulation of money is not the fault of the will. It is the limited *use* you have made of your will that creates your disappointment.

There is nothing wrong with exercising your will for the sake of doing things like accumulating more money. Your problems begin when you exercise your will to make more money so you can experience greater inner freedom, a formula that does not work, because money simply cannot produce a free state of being. The secret is first to understand the unconditional nature of freedom and then exercise your will to experience it, beginning right where you are, regardless of what you do or do not have. By assigning a material value to the condition of freedom and then making your experience of freedom dependent on your possession of that material thing, you effectively close yourself to the possibility of experiencing freedom as long as you lack that thing.

Your Lawn and the Will of God

If you have a lawn, you know that *something* is going to grow in it. What grows in your yard will be determined by your choices. Would you look out over your lawn and say, "Thy will be done?" The natural manifestation process will, of course, produce a potpourri of native plants brought in by the wind, birds, and other wildlife. If this is what you want, fine. In the mountains this is not an uncommon practice. But it is not wrong for you to choose specific grasses, shrubs, flowers, and trees that you want to have in your yard. Exercising your will to make such choices is not a violation of spiritual principles.

Problems and disappointment will arise for you, however, if you plant a particular type of seed or bulb but fully expect to get a different kind of plant. You could not plant tulip bulbs and expect to get daffodils. And yet this is exactly the problem we face in our lives. We *will* into existence conditions and things that we fully expect will produce specific states of being which can only be evolved from within us. When the satisfaction we seek is not forthcoming, we wrongly assume it is our faculty of will that is at fault. What is at fault, however, is our conclusionistic belief that a particular condition of *having* will produce a particular state of *being*.

Charles Fillmore recognized the will as one of our twelve spiritual faculties.[1] When properly focused, this faculty provides us the means by which we carry out God's creative intention. It is not merely the exercise of our will that gets us into trouble. It is our use of the will to accommodate the needs of our limited self-image that causes us problems. We attempt to *will* into manifestation what we think are solutions to problems that, in reality, can only be solved through an expansion of our self-image. When we fail to attain satisfaction in our lives through the exercise of our will, we assume there is another will, a cosmic one, that we must call into play. There is no other will acting outside of us. Our will, at the very deepest level of our being, *is* God's will. The problem is that we have reduced the use of our will to fetching sticks when it is intended to allow us to build the life of our dreams.

The Goal of Your Goal

This brings us to a very important point that I believe is often missed in the goal-setting process. Understanding *where* you are trying to go with your goal-setting activities is the most important key to getting there. I say this because there is often a vast difference between our *stated* goals and our *actual* goals. Our stated goals address our state of *having*—acquisitions, accomplishments, and so on—while our actual goals address our state of *being*. We see the stated goal as the means of accomplishing the actual goal, when in fact it may not. To use Emerson's earlier example, the real reason for the stated goal of going to Naples was to accomplish the actual goal of losing the "sad self." But, as Emerson pointed out, you can manifest your stated goal, that is, you can get to Naples, and still fail to achieve the actual goal of losing the sad self. If you're inclined to be depressed in Los Angeles, chances are good you will eventually become just as depressed in Naples.

It is a clear indication that you are operating from a conclusionistic basis when your stated goals are different than your actual goals. You are saying, in essence, that when you accomplish a particular stated goal—making more money, getting a better job, getting into a new relationship—you will be happy, because then, having acquired this new status, you will be prosperous, successful, or loved. *Having equals being.* It may be true that your current conditions are less than ideal and that some external changes need to be made. To be successful in your goal-setting activities, however, you must first identify your *actual* goal, which always has to do with your state of being, and then begin the process of evolving from within yourself those qualities that are the basis of this goal. This identification of the actual goal will present you with a more direct and probably entirely different course of action. The course of action you would take to get to Naples, for example, is quite different from the course of action you would take to actually lose your sad self.

We all have or have had a "Naples"—some accomplishment, some dream we believed would make us happy if we could just accomplish it. I remember speaking with a man who complained about being completely overrun with responsibilities in his business. "It's funny," he said, "but one of the reasons I wanted to get into business for myself was that I wanted the freedom to be my own man." This man's stated goal, his "Naples," was to be in business for himself. His actual goal was the *freedom to be himself.* He was making his personal freedom dependent on his business going a certain way. This forced him into a manipulative behavior toward his business that only lessened his experience of personal freedom. Trying to make his business produce what only he himself could evolve from within himself forced him into a type of slavery to his business that made him begin to question whether he had made the right decision about going into business for himself.

This man began to resolve his dilemma when I suggested that, right in the midst of his confusion, he begin to make choices that would actually allow him to experience greater freedom. I suggested that he begin seeing himself as already free, instead of thinking his freedom was dependent on the resolution of some situation concerning his business. I suggested that he begin to break the habit of wasting his creative energy by worrying over things he could do nothing about and that he get into the habit of taking immediate action on the things he could. I encouraged him to drop the conclusionistic belief that when his business reached a certain level he could then be happy and free. Instead, I suggested that he think of his business as an evolutionary process. I said he should recognize that new growth meant new challenges, and that resolving challenges was not the objective, but that identifying and releasing his inner blocks to the freedom raised by the challenges were his real objective. In other words, I was suggesting that he use his business, and all the many challenges it provided, to evolve a higher, freer Self. In sharing with him the story of Caleb and the eleven spies, I reminded him that if a challenge looked bigger than he was, it was only an indication he was seeing himself as a grasshopper. The real work was to begin to see himself as an infinite expression of God and then begin to make choices that would bear out this Truth in his daily life.

A Personal Testimony

At one point in my life, many years ago, Unity Village became my "Naples." I was not at all happy with the way my life was going. My musical career was going nowhere. I had, out of necessity, just moved back from Texas to my hometown in northwestern Missouri. To recover from a financial debt incurred in those previous, much leaner years, I had taken work in my family's construction business.

Having discovered Unity Village, I regarded the highlight of my week to be attending the Sunday services, which were, at that time, under the leadership of Sig and Jane Paulson. The services were so rewarding that I didn't mind making the 120-mile round trip through sun, rain, sleet, or snow two, and sometimes three, times a week. The uplift I received in that environment was wonderful, and it gave me something to look forward to in what I otherwise perceived as a rather bland existence. I remember thinking, as do many people, that if I could just live at Unity Village all the time, I could permanently lose my sad self.

One day, as I was drifting along trying to figure out a direction for my life, a very important question occurred to me. Why was it that I could experience such an elevated state of mind at Unity Village but seemed unable to have the same type of experience at home? If this elevated state was coming from within me, as I was told it was, why couldn't I tap into it wherever I was and whatever I was doing?

Pondering this question inspired me to begin arriving early at my work site so I could meditate. I would practice releasing all the negative energy I was putting into my job. I would practice letting go of all the limited preconceptions I was placing on myself while I was on the job. I stopped telling myself I could not be happy in that particular situation. In short, I did a major housecleaning on myself concerning my perception of that experience.

The results were wonderful. Slowly I began to think of that job in an entirely different way. I began to see that nothing but my own restrictive attitude was keeping me from coming fully alive in that situation. I began to have insights and experiences that made me realize that my ability to live life to its fullest was never absent. I was simply sealing it off from my conscious mind by making my desired state of being show a dependency on the presence of certain types of circumstances. This was a case in which I began to bloom where I was planted.

Unnecessary Complications

Because we do not clearly define our actual goals, we are often plagued with a great many complications in our circumstances. If, for example, our stated goal is to enter a loving relationship but our actual goal is to eliminate low self-esteem, we will be forced, as was my businessman friend, into a manipulative type of behavior within the relationship that will most likely erode what self-esteem we do have. If you are in a relationship for the purpose of gaining high self-esteem, you will eventually have to force the relationship to provide you with that desired result. Why? Because even the best relationship is incapable of producing true self-esteem. Of course, others can help to ignite in us the flame of self-esteem. Most of us have had some special person—a parent, a teacher, a spouse, a friend—who believed enough in our ability to encourage us toward some achievement. But it must be *your* flame that is ignited. You cannot live off the flame of another, lest you fall into that spiritually abhorrent condition of dependency.

When your stated goal is to have a loving relationship but your actual goal is to overcome your personal sense of inferiority, you send a mixed message to the Universe. Your self-image, your beliefs, the decisions you make, and your actions influence your circumstantial tendencies twenty-four hours a day. Your true motives will always eventually show up in your life with mechanical precision. You simply cannot escape the consequences of how you see yourself.

If you wish to produce a round shadow, for example, you may do so by holding up a basketball in the sunlight. When you look at the shadow produced by the ball, however, you will notice something else. The shadow of your arm and your entire body is also there. The sun does not respond only to your stated goal of producing a round shadow. It simply shines. Regardless of what your stated objective is, if a shadow-producing object is present, a shadow will be produced.

The Effectiveness of Goal Setting

If goal setting has proven to be a restrictive activity for you, it is not because goal setting itself is restrictive. To the contrary, it may be the effectiveness of goal setting that has presented the greatest problems for you. If you carry an inferiority complex, for example, you will unconsciously set goals that prove you are inferior. An inferiority complex creates an underlying agenda that is just as influential in your circumstantial tendencies as your stated agenda. It is not enough to declare that you have a goal to be rich or healthy or happy. You must make sure your entire agenda is committed to the quality of life you wish. You must also become aware of and release those elements in your consciousness that have kept you from being rich, healthy, and happy in the first place. Goal setting is not just another simple technique of getting something for nothing. You have to be prepared to cleanse yourself of the patterns of thought, feeling, and behavior that have kept you from enjoying the kind of life you want to live. As I indicated in the previous chapter, when you set a major goal for yourself, you are actually agreeing to confront all your deepest fears and inadequacies. You are agreeing to confront and eliminate all the elements in your consciousness that stand between the person you are now and the person you want to be.

Are We Evolving a Strength or Protecting a Weakness?

When it comes to goal setting, the main difference between the evolutionistic thinker and the conclusionistic thinker is that the evolutionist sets goals for the purpose of evolving a particular strength, while the conclusionist tends to set goals for the purpose of protecting a particular weakness. Evolutionists, motivated by the understanding that their purpose in life is to evolve the spiritual attributes which lie unexpressed within their being, do not set out to acquire things for the sake of the things themselves. They use the process of acquisition as a stimulation for further challenge and development. Conclusionistic thinkers, on the other hand, seek to acquire things in order to compensate for conditions of low self-esteem, a sense of powerlessness, or a weak personal identity. Paradoxically, acquisition, from the conclusionistic point of view, ultimately strengthens the very feelings of inadequacy the acquisition was supposed to alleviate in the first place.

There is nothing wrong with using goal-setting techniques to get the things you want in life. But, to quote a Biblical proverb, "To get wisdom is better than gold; to get understanding is to be chosen rather than silver."[2] To use our earlier example, do you want more firewood or do you want more fire? Do you want more things in your life, or do you want a deeper, more meaningful experience? You can, of course, have both. But, as you have undoubtedly demonstrated to yourself already, you can't get to a deeper, more meaningful life through the round-about way of acquiring more things. A deeper, more meaningful experience must itself become the objective, both a stated and an actual goal, and finding it is an inner process.

Summary

1. Happiness is my natural state of being.

2. My will, at the deepest level, is God's will. Every good state of being I desire is unconditionally available to me now.

3. I make sure that my stated goals and my actual goals are one and the same.

4. I make sure that I am using my goals to evolve a new strength, rather than to protect a weakness.

Chapter 10

Understanding the Technique of Tithing

Beyond the Temporal

Considering how important a role the self-image plays in determining our quality of life, it is surprising that apparently so few people factor it into their efforts to live a more prosperous life. It seems the dominating assumption in much of the prosperity-based literature we read is that when, through the use of certain spiritually-based techniques, we learn to solve our temporal problems, we will automatically be happy and our self-image will naturally be lifted to new heights.

A typical illustration might be that of a man who needs a thousand dollars to pay his taxes. He doesn't have it. He reads about the practice of tithing, for example, and how it is a spiritually sound approach to attaining a prosperous life. He decides to try it and before he knows it, almost as if by magic, one thousand dollars appears! An in-law unexpectedly pays a forgotten debt. An unexpected rise in stock values pays a healthy dividend. Unexpected money is found in a checking account. Aunt Betsy dies and leaves him money in her will.

Of course, these things happen. Unfortunately, the use of this kind of example often gives the impression it is merely the application of the technique that produces the solution to life's problems. This tends to foster a very surface, conclusionistic, *doing* kind of approach to creating a prosperous life. That is, if you *do* certain things—if you tithe, visualize abundance, use treasure maps, read prosperity books, attend prosperity workshops, set goals, and say prosperity affirmations every day—you will *have* a full, rich, happy, and prosperous life. As we have seen in the previous chapter and will see again in this and the following chapter, these are all proven methods of influencing, at least to some extent, our circumstantial tendencies. But like any method, the value is determined by whether you approach a particular problem from an evolutionistic or a conclusionistic point of view. You can faithfully apply all these techniques and still manage to maintain the kind of inadequate self-image that ultimately translates into a life of lack and frustration. Every one of these practices, as potentially effective as it can be, is only as effective in producing a high quality experience as your self-image will allow.

☞ Most prosperity books, including this one, will emphasize the practice of giving, for example. But the *act* of giving alone is not what produces a prosperous life. Charles Fillmore, himself a staunch advocate of this practice, observed that "giving with the fear of lack leads to poverty."[1] Why? Because the fear of lack is a self-image issue, and self-image issues cannot be permanently overcome through external actions, not even through a practice as potentially transformative as giving. In determining the quality of your life, the condition of your self-image *always* overrides your actions, regardless of how sincere, well-intentioned, or even spiritually motivated these actions may be.

The effectiveness of any prosperity technique, therefore, *lies in its ability to assist you in making a fundamental shift in the way you see yourself.* If the technique is not being used with this deeper end in mind, it becomes placebo-like in nature and will, at best, produce only sporadic and temporal results. It will fail you in providing the long-term, *sustainable* improvements in the quality of your state of being that you desire. In other words, it is not as much in the *doing* as it is in the self-image you are doing it *from* that makes the difference.

Law and Technique

It is important, then, that we make a distinction between a prosperity law and a prosperity technique. A prosperity law is the underlying, absolute principle that remains true and unchanging, regardless of all appearances to the contrary. There is essentially only one prosperity law, which, as I pointed out in Chapter 3, Charles Fillmore called the "law of infinite expansion." There are, however, many techniques that assist us in complying with this law of infinite expansion. There are techniques that assist us in our finances, relationships, health matters, family life, and choices of employment. God's perfect idea implanted in each of us is, as we have already seen, asserting itself as our impulse to prosper in every one of these areas. In our efforts to prosper, we are only seeking to externalize what is already ours at the deepest levels of our being.

The Role of Technique

Through the application of certain techniques, we can detect, interrupt, and eliminate those elements of our self-image that inhibit the natural, expansive principle of "never-ceasing growth." But the mere application of any technique should *never* be considered a substitute or a means of bypassing the often difficult, sometimes even painful work of identifying and eliminating these ingrained inhibitors. This would be like thinking that a shovel, which is designed to assist you in digging holes, will do the digging for you. When properly understood, the application of a technique can bring to the surface of your mind every identity-related restriction you are now placing on the natural law of expansion. But it is up to you to actually release these restrictions, to change the way you think of yourself and your relationship to the Infinite so this expansion of your self-image may occur. When a technique is used in conjunction with an understanding of this law, it can become a powerful catalyst for change.

Tithing

Though you will often hear it referred to as "the law of tenfold return," tithing is a technique, not a law. As Charles Fillmore implied, not all who give 10 percent of their income experience a tenfold return. Some, because they give out of a consciousness of fear or lack, can actually become 10 percent poorer through their giving. Others, giving out of a consciousness of unlimited abundance, may experience a hundredfold return from their giving. If tithing were a law, everyone who practiced it would always get the same results. When people put two and two together, for instance (and it doesn't matter what the condition of their consciousness is), they will get four. This is a law.

Physicists today say that the outcome of experiments conducted on a subatomic level are greatly influenced by the consciousness of the observer. Apparently the individual belief system of the scientist performing the experiment injects an element of randomness into the outcome of the experiment. The same can be said of tithing. There are many factors that come into play when we tithe. *Self-image, attitude,* and *motivation* are just a few. Because of this, two people can give away 10 percent of their incomes and experience two *completely different results.* If attaining a prosperous life were as simple as writing a check, we would only need to teach tithing. But it is much more complex than this.

Understand that I am, in no way, attempting to undermine the value of the practice of tithing. The point I am making here is that tithing itself, like any other prosperity technique, is not a magic law which will accomplish for you the work that you need to do yourself. When practiced *from a certain mental and emotional disposition,* tithing can *assist* you in complying with the underlying law of infinite expansion. It can, as I said, cause to surface in you a plethora of self-imposed restrictions that have kept you from living the life you could and should be living. Conscious of these restrictions, you can attend to the work of releasing them.

The key word here is *conscious.* It is often said that we should make a habit of tithing. Though it is most effective when practiced with regularity, tithing must *never* become a habit. A habit is an act you can perform *unconsciously*—without thinking. Tithing without thinking and observing what it stirs in you is a futile ritual that only enriches the entity to which you give. It has no more impact on the quality of your life than does the act of writing a check to pay your light bill. You have to be conscious of what a practice like tithing stirs in you. You have to consciously choose the state of being from which you want to give. If your tithing has become habitual, then raise the amount you give to a point where you will once again become *conscious* that you are giving. Only then will the practice become an effective aid in building a prosperity consciousness.

Why Does Tithing Work?

To truly benefit from a technique such as tithing, it is essential you accept, as an absolute given, that you are where you are in life because of the way you have defined yourself. If you wish to experience a more expansive, prosperous life, all the spiritual elements necessary to do so are present. You must release your limited self-image and allow the natural law of expansion to lift you beyond your current attachments. There are a number of ways tithing can help you to accomplish this.

Though money is, in reality, a symbol of universal

substance, it has become much more than this to most of us. Because money does enable us to have and do so many things, we have made it an important aspect of our identity. We have, to a greater or lesser degree, elevated it to a measure of our self-worth. And this is precisely why tithing money in particular can be such a powerful tool of transformation. Giving away something as important as money, especially when there seems to be a scarcity of it, completely goes against the grain of logic of our conclusionistic tendencies. Doing so is seen as a potential depletion of power, identity, and freedom. Having invested this much power and meaning in the money symbol, we can be sure that when we give away as noticeable a portion as 10 percent, it will stir up some feelings in us. *Something* is going to happen.

One of the most important things that can happen through tithing, both in terms of your spiritual development and in improved external conditions, is that the act of giving away something as valued as money will force to the surface of your mind the *real* issues which keep you from experiencing a more prosperous life. Tithing will trigger in you all your misplaced attachments to things, every fear of lack, any lack of faith in the Invisible as your source of supply, and so on. As you acknowledge and release these blockages, you experience an improved state of being *and* the inevitable consequence of a more prosperous state of affairs.

Obviously then, there is a condition attached to making tithing, or any technique for that matter, an effective practice. You must take the time to observe these "stirrings" as they occur in you, and then you must commit yourself to doing something with them, once you become aware of them. You have to bring your limited self-image more into alignment with the image of God that you are. This often requires some deep, soul-searching work, a great deal of letting go, a lot of affirmation work, and, perhaps most important, a commitment to the long haul. Just as there is no antidepressant drug that can eliminate the cause of depression, there is no quick and easy way to sidestep the issue of an inadequate, lack-producing self-image. The application of every technique must be accompanied by a self-administered release and affirmation therapy, if you will, with the goal of identifying and eliminating all spiritually inhibiting aspects of your self-image. Every fear and internal sense of inadequacy that you have been trying to resolve with money and other external means must first be resolved within yourself, by you. Until you understand this, your efforts to prosper through the application of any technique will produce temporary results, at best.

An Exercise: Release and Affirmation

Tithing is most effective when it is used as a premeditated method of bringing to the surface of your mind all your dysfunctional supply issues. When you sit down to write your tithe check, make this a quiet time to observe what goes on in you as you prepare your gift. Do you feel reluctant to give? What is the source of your reluctance? Do you fear the act of tithing will deplete you? Are you recognizing that God is the unlimited source of your supply? Are you prepared to make decisions and take action beyond tithing to demonstrate that God is your unlimited source? Is your gift accompanied by uncertainty? Do you feel weakened by giving? Then take this opportunity to release your fear and weakness and endow your gift with the strength and confidence of your true Self. Let these qualities quietly rise in you. Do not give your gift until you can give it in trust and in confidence that, as an unlimited expression of God, your unfailing source, your greater supply of all good is assured.

If you find there are negative feelings arising in you as you prepare your gift, a simple statement of release like this one may be helpful:

I now release all fear of lack and uncertainty about giving this gift.

Take a moment to actually release your negative

feelings. Then follow your statement of release with an affirmation such as this one:

God is my unfailing source. I freely give this gift knowing I can never deplete God. I am peaceful, free, and completely expectant of greater good through my giving.

When you achieve the feeling described in this affirmation, give your gift, then completely release it. If, after you have given, the old feelings begin to well up in you once again, repeat the denial and the affirmation, seeking again to achieve the feelings they describe. You will maximize the impact of your giving, because you will be using this technique as a means for evolving in yourself a new, more prosperous state of being.

Whatever technique you are using, whether it be tithing, treasure mapping, list making, goal setting, affirming, or visualizing, be sure to observe closely what these practices stir in you. Most important, be ready and willing to release your fears and evolve new strengths. I use all these techniques in various kinds of situations, depending on what I feel will be most helpful under the circumstances. But I always use them with the understanding that they are not designed to do the work for me. They are designed to help me focus my attention on those areas where the work needs to be done.

Summary

1. There is only one prosperity law, *the law of infinite expansion.* There are many techniques that can assist me in complying with this law of infinite expansion.

2. The effectiveness of every prosperity technique lies in its ability to assist me in making a fundamental shift in the way I see and feel about myself.

3. Each time I practice a prosperity technique, I will be conscious of what it stirs in me. I will release those feelings which inhibit my growth, and I will affirm those feelings which enhance it.

Chapter 11

Consciously Using Your Imagination

What Is Creative Visualization?

In the previous chapter, I mentioned the additional techniques of creative visualization and treasure mapping. Both of these are techniques you will nearly always see associated with the concept of prosperity. In simple terms, the technique of creative visualization is a *consciously directed* use of the imaging faculty of the mind—the faculty of imagination—to attain a thing, condition, or quality of life you desire. The idea is that if you hold a clear picture in your mind of what it is you want to experience in your life, that picture will manifest itself in time.

Treasure mapping is a more graphic version of creative visualization, involving the creation of a poster full of actual pictures that represent the things you desire. It is a more physical, hands-on approach to the mental technique of visualization. Because the principles that apply to both practices are identical and because I so rarely employ the use of treasure mapping, I will confine the focus of this chapter to the single term *creative visualization*. For a more indepth look into the treasure mapping technique, I would suggest reading Mary Katherine Mac-Dougall's booklet *What Treasure Mapping Can Do for You*,[1] available through Unity School of Christianity.

A Look at the Imagination

Since I am defining *creative visualization* as a consciously directed use of the imagination, I want to begin with a discussion of this important faculty. Over the years I have come to believe that the imagination is probably one of the most misunderstood, misused, and yet most powerful and influential faculties we possess. Though it is usually portrayed in this way, it is not the highest function of the imagination to create an image of that prosperous person we want to become. The highest function of the imagination is to *receive from within* the image of the true Self that is the living force behind our natural impulse to prosper. As we have seen, the imagination is certainly capable of creating and sustaining a self-image. But the self-image it has created is the "grasshopper" self that has gotten us into the condition of limitation in the first place. Much of our work lies in cleaning up the mess made by an unbridled and misunderstood imagination.

As I have indicated throughout this book, the person you want to become is not a product of your imagination. It is the product of the eternal, Cosmic process. The first and highest function of the imagination is to serve as a kind of aperture through which your true Self emerges into your consciousness. As this emergence of your true Self occurs, the imagination literally becomes flushed with new possibilities, new ways of seeing and experiencing life. Often I go within in quiet meditation with the single purpose of opening this secret aperture to my true Self. The result is that my mind becomes flooded with so many creative ideas that I could not possibly act on them all. We are literally fueled by a living current of intelligent and creative energy that stands waiting to bubble forth into our open minds. An imagination that taps into this source of energy is an imagination functioning at its best.

Unfortunately, the technique of creative visualization is often restricted to solving our temporal problems. You want a better job, so you visualize yourself in a better job. You want a new car, so you visualize yourself in a new car. You want a better golf game, so you visualize yourself as a better putter. These are all legitimate uses of the technique of creative visualization, and I am not suggesting that we abandon them. Studies show that simply holding a clear vision of yourself accomplishing or improving on a thing can actually produce dramatic and favorable results. I, for one, would much rather improve my skills in this fashion than submit to hours of instruction.

But if we are after a richer quality of life, a level of prosperity both enduring and deeply satisfying, our focus must eventually be placed on that person sitting at a desk on a new job, that person sitting behind the wheel of a new car, and that person doing the putting out on a golf course. In other words, we don't want to limit our use of the technique of creative visualization to accumulating bigger stacks of firewood. We want to use it to start a fire!

A Case in Point

Let me give you an illustration of the importance of placing our imaginative focus on the person behind our myriad of desires. Some years ago I was teaching a class based on the book *Creative Visualization* by Shakti Gawain—a book, by the way, that I highly recommend. During the course of our discussion, the subject of world peace was raised. A woman, pointing through the classroom window to her car in the parking lot, called our attention to her bumper sticker, which read, "Visualize World Peace." "This is what we all need to do," she declared.

To emphasize a point I was trying to make in the

class, I seized the opportunity and asked her this simple question: "Are you now at peace with the world as it is?"

Her response was revealing. She said: "Of course I'm not at peace with the world as it is. The world is a dangerous and violent place!" The emotion of her conviction flashed in her eyes as she spoke.

Something very significant occurred to me as the result of this woman's response. Like many, she desired a world of peace. However, the actual vision she held of our world was that it was a "dangerous and violent place." Her desired vision of world peace was something that *could* possibly take place in the future. Her negative vision, however, was taking place in *real time.*

The significance of this fact lies in understanding that *it is the real-time images we hold which determine the quality of our experience.* This woman was relating to the world on a day-to-day basis as if it were a dangerous and violent place. That was her definition and her expectation of the world. How could the world show her anything else if that is how she chose to define it? If this woman truly wanted to create an impact through her visualization of world peace, she would have to abort her real-time, negative vision and replace it with a vision of the world as a peaceful place!

Now, this is not merely an exercise in semantics or

an attempt to smooth over the challenges we en-counter in life. This woman was demonstrating a perfect example of conclusionistic thinking as it re-lated to the technique of creative visualization. She reasoned that if enough people would visualize world peace, then eventually we would have it. She was making the assumption that the condition of the world at present, or the behavior of its inhabi-tants, was responsible for blocking our access to the experience of peace. In truth, peace is never ab-sent; it is only obscured by our own visions of the world as a dangerous and violent place. It is the prin-ciple embodied in these words attributed to Jesus: "Do you not say, 'There are yet four months, then comes the harvest'? I tell you, lift up your eyes, and see how the fields are already white for harvest."[2]

Granted, the peace I am speaking of is a peace that typically surpasses the conventional understanding of the word. The peace of which I speak is a perma-nent peace that is accessible to us even in the midst of life's most violent of storms. It is the type of peace that Jesus was speaking of when he said: "Peace I leave with you; my peace I give to you. I do not give to you as the world gives. Do not let your hearts be troubled, and do not let them be afraid."[3] If we, as in-dividuals and as a people, are to make true spiritual progress on this planet, we must understand that this permanent peace is always present, always ac-cessible, always ready to be "harvested." The experience of real and lasting peace does not depend on the elimination of things like war or crime. Jesus inhabited one of the most violent regions in the world, yet he spoke of the accessibility of peace. The experience of inner peace is, rather, a matter of choice, a matter of lifting our vision to the higher realms of this great, invisible cosmic ocean that we inhabit. We can only bring this kind of peace into our external world by first laying hold of the condition of permanent peace within ourselves.

I have encountered many who are out there trying to rid the world of its apparent multitude of evils. It has been my observation that these people are often conducting their crusade from a wounded and inadequate self-image. Their causes may indeed be noble. But it is a spiritual law that we cannot create conditions which are healthier than we are, no matter how many people we have supporting us in our endeavor. I have to agree with Thoreau when he wrote, "There are a thousand hacking at the branches of evil to one who is striking at the root."[4] We do not heal our own wounds and feelings of inadequacy by striking at the multitude of branches of all the apparent injustices of the world. We strike at the root of life's challenges by first placing ourselves on higher inner ground. Our healing comes through unleashing our own spiritual wholeness from within, letting that wholeness completely engulf this little, hacking "grasshopper" self that is the product of our own limited vision. As we allow this true vision of ourselves to unfold through our consciousness, our relationship to our world is lifted to heights our "grasshopper" vision could never hope to behold.

The Vision You Feel

When we think of the technique of creative visualization, we may be tempted to think only in terms of mental pictures. Visualization is, after all, associated with the act of seeing, whether it be with the eye of the flesh or the eye of the mind. The most powerful aspect of any vision, however, is the *feeling* it arouses in you. In my first book, *A Practical Guide to Meditation and Prayer,* I wrote about an experience that had a profound impact on my life, an impact which continues to this day. I also wrote about this experience in the song "Something Spoke to Me," which appears on my second CD, *Vision of Hope.* Here is how I describe that experience in the song:

> One day in my life—many years ago—
> A heavenly vision it came.
> I saw the great depths of the human soul,
> And since then I've not been the same.[5]

This experience, as the lyrics say, was truly a vision. But I saw nothing. It was what I *felt* that left its transforming mark on me. I felt absolutely whole,

completely embraced and supported by an unconditional love that extends far beyond my ability to
describe. I completely understand what Carl Jung
was talking about when he wrote: "I could not say I
believe. I know! I have had the experience of being
gripped by something that is stronger than myself,
something that people call God."[6]

I carry a beautiful vision for my life, but I do not
see where this vision is leading me. I *feel* where it is
leading me. If ten years ago someone were to ask me
to describe to them what my life would look like
today, I would have painted a very different picture
from what my life is like now. The feeling of knowing
that my life would get better and better, however,
has always been absolutely accurate. I have come to
know, perhaps against the grain of conventional wisdom, that *you don't have to see where you are going
to be able to get there.* I am convinced that the highest, most accurate form of life navigation is conducted at the feeling level of our being. I am not
saying that we should be controlled by our emotions. Those who are controlled by their emotions
are usually out of control. What I am saying is that
the person, the being, you want to become is now
pressing through you, making itself known to you at
the organic, feeling level. Call it "intuition." Call it
whatever you wish. But if you will make this deep
feeling the basis of your life's vision, the basis for

every major decision you make, you will prosper beyond any image you will ever intentionally throw up on the screen of your mind.

An Exercise: Creative Visualization

I bring this chapter to a close by suggesting a simple meditative exercise that could lead to some wonderful, even dramatic changes in your life. You will need a writing pad and pen or pencil. Sit comfortably in a quiet place and allow your body to relax. I am going to ask you to respond to two simple instructions. Read them carefully and then write your responses, taking as much time as you need. In fact, I suggest that you work with this exercise over a period of several days, refining your responses until you are absolutely certain they accurately describe your feelings.

1. Describe the feelings you would have if you were now expressing yourself as the person you know you can become.

2. Describe the feelings you would have for your life if it were now the life you dream of having.

Embodied in your responses is the level and quality of experience that is accessible to you. When you are satisfied with what you have written, allow yourself, again in a meditative setting, to experience the feelings you describe in your responses. Do not try to *make* anything happen. Simply bask in the warmth, the excitement, the pleasure, the fulfillment of these feelings. Spend about ten or fifteen minutes a day allowing these feelings to arise. In addition, as you go about your daily tasks, recall these feelings from time to time, allowing yourself to experience them in the midst of your workday or while on the phone, doing the dishes, or mowing the lawn.

This simple exercise is a very highly effective form of creative visualization. Don't use it to try to change yourself or your world. Simply watch yourself and your life take on these qualities you agree to express.

Summary

1. It is not the highest function of the imagination to create an image of that prosperous person we want to become. The highest function of the imagination is to receive from within the image of the true Self that is the living force behind our natural impulse to prosper.

2. It is the real-time images we hold that determine the quality of our experience. It is a spiritual law that we cannot create conditions

which are healthier than the image we hold of ourselves.

3. The most powerful aspect of any vision you hold is the feeling it arouses in you. You don't have to see where you are going to get there. You need only feel it. The highest, most accurate form of life navigation is conducted at the feeling level of our being.

Chapter 12

Bringing It All Together

One Day at a Time

When we talk about the process of changing ourselves, which is what this book is all about, we are talking about changing our values. We stay where we are in life for as long as we see some value in doing so. Until we see the value in making a change in our self-image, our belief system, the types of decisions we make, and the actions we take, it is not likely that we will move on to a new, more prosperous state of being and lifestyle.

We worry, for example, because we see some value, some benefit in doing so. We may intellectually come to grips with the fact that worry accomplishes nothing, that it is just a bad and useless habit. But we will continue to do it, because in some strange way we still think it is something we need to do. We cannot build up a big enough inventory of external assets to free us from worry, as long as we see some value in doing it.

Negative mental and emotional activities like worry are habitual reactions to a certain kind of external appearance. Breaking such habits is not an easy thing to do, especially if you have engaged in practicing them for most of your adult life. You may recognize the valuelessness of such a habit and decide that you are going to rid yourself of it once and for all and that you're going to do it right now! Two hours later, however, you're doing it again, as strongly as ever.

Understanding the value we place on our habits is the key to changing them. I quit smoking the moment that doing so was no longer a valuable asset to the identity I carried. Though giving up the external habit was an instantaneous change, beneath that change was an evolution from one self-image to another. It's a little like the movie star who took twenty years to become an overnight success.

The point I am making here is that there are no restrictions placed on the speed at which you build your new and prosperous life. You move forward at the exact rate at which you are willing to let go. You cannot force a prosperous external life without the improved self-image to sustain it. As Emerson wrote: "A political victory, a rise of rents, the recovery of your sick or the return of your absent friend, or some other favorable event raises your spirits, and you think good days are preparing for you. Do not

believe it. Nothing can bring you peace but yourself."[1] We often get excited when, through the application of some prosperity technique—a series of affirmations, for example—we see immediate changes
in a particular circumstance. While this is a good
and desirable result, it is, more than likely, a non-
sustainable quirk that has little to do with the overall improvement of your circumstantial tendencies.
In a few days' time, you may apply that same set of
affirmations to a similar type of situation, only to
find it has no apparent impact at all.

We simply cannot force the quality of our circumstantial tendencies past the envelope of our self-
image. It is, in my opinion, better to strap yourself in
for the long haul than it is to think that, because
you've had a few amazing demonstrations, your life
is going to be just as you want it by sometime next
week. You and I are *evolving* toward our spiritually
refined Self, a process that has probably been going
on for a lot longer than any of us can imagine. We
need to keep our focus on the long-term investment,
so to speak, enjoying all the many wonderful demonstrations we see along the way, but not allowing ourselves either to be too elated with our successes or
to completely fall apart every time we encounter
some apparent setback.

All the work that you and I have to do is laid before us each moment of each day. We are only re-

quired to be aware of how we are relating to events in our life right now. If we are relating to these events from the old, worn-out set of values, then we catch ourselves realizing this way is no longer sufficient for us. If we are in a job we do not like, for example, and we find ourselves sitting at our desk thinking about how much we do not like it, we realize the value-lessness and ineffectiveness of such thinking and we begin, in that moment, to take a more constructive approach. We remember that we are not limited by the job. We are limited only by the way we see ourselves in that job. We begin the work of changing the way we see ourselves by evolving a new state of being. We are successful in life to the degree that we are successful in the moment. Moment to moment, we build a more prosperous life.

Summary

To bring it all together, living a prosperous life asks that we be willing to find a deeper experience of our true Self. We are really happy only to the extent that we are true to our spiritual natures and are actively involved in the pursuit of our dreams. Living our lives solely for material acquisitions will fail us, because things and even accomplishments do not have the power to bring lasting satisfaction.

The external world cannot provide the prosperous life our souls crave. We must acquire it from within, evolve it from the inside out. Our feelings of lack and inadequacy stem from trying to be something that we are not.

There is a living force within us compelling us to expand into a higher quality of life. This force is the voice of God. It is at the heart of all our desires and is why "following our bliss" does bring us to our true vocation. To discover it, we must meditate and listen to the guidance we receive.

Our current work may put a roof over our head, but if we are not passionate about it, it is not the best thing we could be doing. Doing what we love is not easy, nor is it a quick fix. It will ask a great deal of us, but the rewards of pursuing it far outweigh any struggle we will encounter.

Who we usually think we are, the self-image we maintain, is not who we truly are, in essence. It is not our Self. Most prosperity attempts go awry because we try to prosper our limited self-image, rather than the true spiritual being that we are. We are *conclusionistic* in our thinking, living as if *having equals being.*

Material prosperity alone cannot prosper us, because it is never enough. But it is a natural by-product of our Self-discovery and Self-expression. Everything we try to achieve through material acquisition has a spiritual counterpart that already exists as an integral part of our true Self. Our prosperity comes from an *evolutionistic* approach of *evolving* from within ourselves that which God *involved* in us from the beginning.

We all have circumstantial tendencies that get in the way of this evolution. They are a combination of our limited self-image, our belief system, our decisions, and our actions. We really only can change these tendencies by *changing the way we see ourselves.*

As we change, the weaker and stronger elements of our self-image clash. We often experience that the things we fear most come upon us. It is crucial that we not be daunted by this but, instead, welcome the release of our weaker elements. To change our habits, we must initiate new behaviors and not allow ourselves to be stopped by the fear of change.

Goal setting, tithing, creative visualization (and treasure mapping) can be effective techniques for mastering the one prosperity law, the law of infinite expansion. This law states that there is a never-ending growth, evolution, and expression of God's perfect idea within creation. This "perfect idea" is available to us each moment.

Our real work is to change how we relate to ourselves and our world, to experience the higher vision of this perfect idea, and to allow the prosperous life to flow to us, through us, and from us. This is living the prosperous life.

Notes

All Bible translations are from the Revised Standard Version, unless otherwise noted.

Introduction

1. Henry David Thoreau, in Bartlett's *Familiar Quotations*, 15th ed., Little, Brown and Company, Boston, 1980, p. 558.

Chapter 1   The Essence of Prosperity

1. The Gospel of Thomas is part of a collection of Gnostic writings discovered in Nag Hammadi, Egypt, in 1947. Many scholars believe The Gospel of Thomas served as a source document for Matthew, Mark, and Luke.

2. Jesus Christ, Saying #74, from The Gospel of Thomas in James M. Robinson's *The Nag Hammadi Library*, Harper & Row, New York, 1977, p. 126.

3. Ralph Waldo Emerson, in Newton Dillaway's *The Gospel of Emerson*, Unity Books, Unity Village, Mo., 1990, p. 19.

4. Luke 9:25 NRSV.

5. Luke 6:48–49.

6. Thoreau, p. 560.

Chapter 2   The Foundation for Lasting Prosperity

1. Ibid., p. 559.

2. Ralph Waldo Emerson, *Emerson's Essays*, Thomas Y. Crowell Company, New York, 1951, p. 217.

3. Doug Bottorff, *Vision of Hope* (CD), Unity Multimedia, Unity Village, Mo., 1998.

4. Ibid.

5. Ibid.

Chapter 3   The Law of Infinite Expansion

1. H. Emilie Cady, *Complete Works of H. Emilie Cady,* Unity Books, Unity Village, Mo., 1995, p. 38.

2. Charles Fillmore, *The Revealing Word,* Unity Books, Unity Village, Mo., p. 119.

3. Matthew 6:33.

Chapter 5   Understanding Your Motivation to Prosper

1. H. Emilie Cady, *Lessons in Truth,* Unity Books, Unity Village, Mo., 1995, p. 111.

2. Emerson, *Emerson's Essays* pp. 59–60.

3. John 5:2–15.

Chapter 6   The Evolutionistic Approach

1. Fillmore, p. 65.

2. Revelation 3:20.

Chapter 7   Changing Your Circumstantial Tendencies

1. Exodus 3:8.

2. Numbers 13:30.

3. Numbers 13:33.

Chapter 8   Meeting the Dynamics of Challenge

1. Job 3:25.

Chapter 9   Setting Your Goal and Letting Go

1. Charles Fillmore, *The Twelve Powers of Man,* Unity Books, Unity Village, Mo., 1995, p. 13. The twelve spiritual fac-

ulties are as follows: faith, strength, wisdom, love, power, imagination, understanding, will, order, zeal, renunciation, and life.

2. Proverbs 16:16.

Chapter 10   Understanding the Technique of Tithing

1. Fillmore, *The Revealing Word,* p. 159.

Chapter 11   Consciously Using Your Imagination

1. Katherine MacDougall, *What Treasure Mapping Can Do for You,* Unity School of Christianity, Unity Village, Mo., 1968.

2. John 4:35.

3. John 14:27 NRSV.

4. Thoreau, p. 559.

5. Bottorff.

6. Carl Jung, in *Peter's Quotations: Ideas for Our Time,* William Morrow and Company, New York, 1977, p. 220.

Chapter 12   Bringing It All Together

1. Emerson, in Newton Dillaway's *The Gospel of Emerson,* p. 75.

About the Author

J. Douglas Bottorff, ordained in 1981, has served Unity ministries in Kansas City, Missouri; Bay City, Michigan; Springfield, Missouri; and now in Evergreen, Colorado.

Doug is the author of *A Practical Guide to Meditation and Prayer* and of many articles in *Unity Magazine* since 1983. He also was a contributing writer to Sir John Marks Templeton's *Discovering the Laws of Life*. In addition to writing and speaking, he enjoys writing, performing, and recording music with a New Thought/metaphysical Christian message. His CD/cassette albums include *One World* and *Vision of Hope*.

Doug is married to Elizabeth and is the father of two grown children, Ashley and Audrey.

More down-to-earth advice on inner guidance

A Practical Guide to
Meditation
and Prayer

by J. Douglas Bottorff

Add a fuller, richer dimension
to your spiritual life as you combine
meditation and prayer in daily practice.
*What is the difference between
meditation and prayer?*
Why is each important?
How can I meditate effectively?
In this enlightening book, Bottorff answers these
and other questions about the often misunderstood
yet vital spiritual practices of meditation and prayer.
He offers original, challenging, and practical insights
into the how, why, theory, and practice and application
of meditation and prayer. He lays the foundation for
positive experience and shows how to apply it to the
daily practices of prayer and meditation.

Learn how to make meditation and prayer
important parts of your day, and enjoy the success
and enlightenment they bring!

$9.95
A Practical Guide to Meditation and Prayer, #108
ISBN 0-87159-036-0, softcover, 143 pp.
To order call (816) 969-2069 or 1-800-669-0282
Or write: Unity Books and Multimedia Publishing
    1901 NW Blue Parkway
    Unity Village, MO 64065-0001

Printed in the U.S.A.   117–1768–10M–8-98